Key Topics in Counselling Psychology

I0421917

This accessible and engaging text introduces the reader to the history and development of counselling psychology before outlining its values, ways of working (therapeutically and when engaging with research), and other key areas.

It promotes the diverse ways that counselling psychologists engage with individuals and the wider communities in which they work and serve, and in doing so, emphasises the core philosophical thinking that commonly underpins the work of counselling psychologists in therapy, research, education, or other leadership roles. Through practical examples and reflexive questions, this book highlights the roots of the discipline in value-based ethics and humanistic thinking, then explores the important psychological theories informing counselling psychology practice. These include the core therapeutic theories underpinning psychodynamic, cognitive behavioural, and humanistic therapies, and also contributions from intersectionality, social justice, and ecological systems approaches. Following a section on research methodology, this book goes on to look at the impact of counselling psychology across society and the avenues for further development.

It is core reading for students in counselling psychology as well as those training in therapeutic disciplines such as counselling or psychotherapy.

Terry Hanley is a Professor of Counselling Psychology at the University of Manchester. He is a Health and Care Professions Council (HCPC)-registered Practitioner Psychologist and a Fellow of the British Psychological Society (BPS). He has written widely around therapeutic theory and research, including co-editing *The SAGE Handbook of Counselling and Psychotherapy* (with Dr Laura Winter).

Laura Anne Winter is a BPS Fellow and Chartered Psychologist, an HCPC-registered Counselling Psychologist, and a Reader in Counselling Psychology and Education based at the University of Manchester. She has co-edited several textbooks previously, including *The Handbook of Social Justice in Psychological Therapies* (with Professor Divine Charura) and *The SAGE Handbook of Counselling and Psychotherapy* (with Professor Terry Hanley).

BPS Key Topics in Psychology

British Psychological Society

Routledge, in partnership with the British Psychological Society (BPS), is pleased to present *BPS Key Topics in Psychology*, a series of short introductory books that focus on a specific field within psychology. Each book is broken down into bitesize chunks to provide a helpful overview of core psychology topics, made clear by a five-part structure: foundations, theories, methodologies, impacts, and emerging areas. Written by active and experienced authors, these essential books encourage students to approach fundamental concepts with confidence and critical thinking.

Books may incorporate student-friendly pedagogies, including tools such as: feature boxes; key terms and definitions; and links to further reading online. Concise yet comprehensive, these books offer a simple and accessible overview of core psychology topics for students looking for a summary of key concepts in the topic, or those new to the area.

Key Topics in Educational Psychology
Lisa Marks Woolfson

Key Topics in Forensic Psychology
Terri Cole and Dara Mojtahedi

Key Topics in Children's Emotional Development
Dale Hay

Key Topics in Attitude and Persuasion
Wojciech Cwalina and Paweł Koniak

Key Topics in Counselling Psychology
Terry Hanley and Laura Anne Winter

For more information about this series, please visit: www.routledge.com/ BPS-Key-Topics-in-Psychology/book-series/BPSKTP.

Key Topics in Counselling Psychology

Terry Hanley and
Laura Anne Winter

Routledge
Taylor & Francis Group

LONDON AND NEW YORK

Designed cover image: getty images

First published 2026
by Routledge
4 Park Square, Milton Park, Abingdon, Oxon OX14 4RN

and by Routledge
605 Third Avenue, New York, NY 10158

Routledge is an imprint of the Taylor & Francis Group, an informa business

© 2026 Terry Hanley and Laura Anne Winter

The right of Terry Hanley and Laura Anne Winter to be identified as authors of this work has been asserted in accordance with sections 77 and 78 of the Copyright, Designs and Patents Act 1988.

All rights reserved. No part of this book may be reprinted or reproduced or utilised in any form or by any electronic, mechanical, or other means, now known or hereafter invented, including photocopying and recording, or in any information storage or retrieval system, without permission in writing from the publishers.

For Product Safety Concerns and Information please contact our EU representative GPSR@taylorandfrancis.com. Taylor & Francis Verlag GmbH, Kaufingerstraße 24, 80331 München, Germany.

Trademark notice: Product or corporate names may be trademarks or registered trademarks, and are used only for identification and explanation without intent to infringe.

British Library Cataloguing-in-Publication Data
A catalogue record for this book is available from the British Library

ISBN: 9781032935171 (hbk)
ISBN: 9781032902494 (pbk)
ISBN: 9781003546733 (ebk)

DOI: 10.4324/9781003546733

Typeset in Galliard
by codeMantra

Access the Support Material: www.routledge.com/9781032902494

In memory of Clare Lennie.

Contents

Acknowledgements

First, thank you to Lucy Kennedy at Routledge for involving us in this series. Thanks also to colleagues who reviewed and provided valuable feedback on various chapters on the way: Divine Charura, Ola Demkowicz, and Rachel Tribe. Whilst we take responsibility for the final words that we have written, your thoughtful engagement with the book has certainly helped to strengthen this it.

Terry
To all the colleagues and friends at the University of Manchester and within the field of counselling psychology.
To Becky, Arthur, Matilda, and Wilf.
To Laura, for being brill as per usual.

Laura
Thanks to the University of Manchester Academic Returners' Scheme (and Rachel Cowen for the creation of this fantastic initiative) for providing some much-needed time post-maternity leave to write.
Thanks also to Terry for the chats about what counselling psychology is and can be, help with my awful referencing, and more generally being a great colleague to collaborate with.
To Jack, Rosa, Cerys, and Owen: thanks for the chaos, the joy, and all the learning together.
Finally, to the counselling psychology community: the trainees past and present, amazing colleagues both at Manchester and beyond, thank you.

Introduction

Welcome and purpose of the book

First, welcome and thank you for deciding to take a look. This book has been written as an invitation to step into the evolving world of counselling psychology. As its title suggests, it aims to introduce what we believe to be some of the key issues facing counselling psychology at this point in time. Rather than acting as a technical manual or an exhaustive overview, it offers an introduction to key philosophies, theories, research, and practices that are currently shaping the field. Whilst as authors we are based in the United Kingdom, it is likely to have international relevance, given the global nature of psychology as a discipline. It is designed to support those who are beginning or continuing to think about how psychology can be applied in ways that support not just the alleviation of distress but also growth, justice, and meaningful connection.

Counselling psychology is rooted in values that honour the complexity and messiness of people's lives. This includes acknowledging that psychological well-being and distress are shaped not only by individual experiences but also by our varying social, relational, political, and cultural contexts. Whilst the discipline draws on psychological theory and research, it is also deeply concerned with ethics, reflexivity, and the quality of human relationships. This book reflects this spirit, and it invites the readers to reflect upon their own experiences in relation to the subject matter and recognises that psychological work is not separate from the world we live in.

Throughout the chapters that follow, we have attempted to connect with some of the wide range of perspectives and voices present in the world of counselling psychology. Some of these reflect long-standing traditions in the profession whilst others highlight areas where counselling psychology is beginning to stretch, challenge itself, and reimagine its role. Together, they build a picture of a profession that is diverse, responsive, and continually evolving. Our hope is that this book encourages curiosity,

DOI: 10.4324/9781003546733-1

thoughtful engagement, and a sense of connection with the ideas and practices that counselling psychologists bring into the world.

Who this book is for

Fundamentally, this book is for anyone who is beginning to wonder what it means to work psychologically with people. It is for those who want to better understand how psychologists can support others through difficult experiences, and how such work is shaped by culture, society, values, and relationships. You may be curious about therapeutic work, interested in research in this area, drawn to the idea of helping others, or simply interested in how psychological ideas can be applied beyond theory. Wherever you are coming from, this book will hopefully have plenty of food for thought around all these areas.

You might be reading this as part of your studies towards a purely academic qualification, during your training to become a therapist or applied psychologist, or simply because you want to explore the ideas further – indeed, you might have been a qualified counselling psychologist for several years but want to engage further with recent writing and ideas. Whatever your path, we hope this book meets you with openness and invites you into dialogue with the questions it raises. You are not expected to have all the answers; we certainly don't, and this book does not aim to provide them. In fact, much of counselling psychology begins with learning to sit with uncertainty, to listen closely, and to ask better questions. Our aim is to help you begin to do just that.

Structure of the book

This book is organised into five parts, each designed to introduce key areas of counselling psychology in a clear and accessible way. Whilst these chapters can be read in sequence, they are also intended to stand alone, allowing readers to explore topics in the order that feels most relevant or interesting to them.

The first part of the book, *Key Foundations*, introduces the origins and guiding principles of counselling psychology. Rather than starting with technical definitions, it explores the historical roots, philosophical assumptions, and core values that shape the discipline. Together, *Chapter 1: Origins and Purpose* and *Chapter 2: Philosophy, Values, and Ethics* lay the groundwork for understanding how counselling psychologists think about people, distress, and change.

The second part, *Key Theories*, focuses on the schools of thought that inform the work of counselling psychologists. *Chapter 3: Thinking about Therapy* reflects upon the dominant theories that counselling psychologists make use of in their therapeutic work, whilst *Chapter 4: Thinking about Systems* considers how psychologists engage with the socio-political systems around us. *Chapter 5: Thinking about Leadership* then looks at how they take up roles of influence and responsibility within wider organisational and social contexts, and how they might be informed by their counselling psychology values and disrupt existing practices.

The third part of the book, *Key Methodologies*, introduces the research landscape and explores how counselling psychologists engage with different methodological approaches that are ethically grounded, contextually aware, and socially meaningful. This section includes three chapters that reflect different but complementary approaches to research. These are *Chapter 6: Doing Pluralistic Research*, *Chapter 7: Doing Reflexive Research*, and *Chapter 8: Doing Transformative Research*. Together, these chapters highlight the profession's commitment to research that is rigorous, reflexive, and capable of contributing to individual, systemic, and societal transformation.

The fourth part, *Key Impacts*, looks at how counselling psychologists contribute meaningfully across a range of contexts. This section includes *Chapter 9: Impacting Individuals and Services*, which focuses upon the ways that counselling psychologists might support change for those who access services and how they can become proactively involved in service development, and *Chapter 10: Impacting Communities and Policy*, which expands the lens to consider broader social engagement, advocacy, and the influence of counselling psychologists on policy and systemic change.

The fifth and final part, *Key Emerging Areas*, explores issues that are likely to receive increasing attention in the coming years. *Chapter 11: Developing Ecosystems of Support and Learning* considers how psychologists can coordinate and enhance wider networks of support, whilst *Chapter 12: Increasing Anti-oppressive Practices* examines the growing focus on social justice and the political nature of our roles and practices.

Across the book, you'll find reflection activities, accessible summaries, and suggestions for further reading and resources. These are included not just to aid learning but also to invite you into a more engaged and curious relationship with the material.

A note on language and accessibility

Throughout this book, care has been taken to try to use language that is clear, inclusive, and accessible. Counselling psychology is a thoughtful and often complex field, and with that comes the use of specialised terms and concepts. Rather than assuming prior knowledge, this book introduces key ideas gradually and uses language that is designed to support learning.

When specific or technical terms appear, such as *reflexivity, epistemology*, or *diagnostic frameworks*, they are presented in **bold** and defined in boxes throughout. This allows you to revisit and make sense of these concepts as you go, without disrupting the flow of reading. The aim is not to simplify the ideas, but to make them more approachable and easier to engage with over time.

Language also plays a powerful role in shaping how we think about people, place, identity, and psychological distress. In writing this book, attention has been paid to how language can either reinforce or challenge assumptions about mental health and well-being, social identities, and support. Care has been taken to try and use respectful and thoughtful terminology throughout, whilst also acknowledging that language is constantly evolving and that we may not always get it right. This book is written with humility and a willingness to learn, and readers are encouraged to engage critically and compassionately with all its content, including the language used.

Finally, this book encourages active engagement. You are invited to pause, reflect, and return to ideas more than once. Accessibility, in this sense, is not just about the words used but about making space for different ways of learning, questioning, and thinking critically.

Introducing the authors

In counselling psychology, who we are matters. Our identities, values, and experiences shape how we understand the world, how we relate to others, and how we engage with knowledge. This is known as **positionality**). With this in mind, we provide a brief snapshot of who we are here to help give a flavour of the worlds that we live in and the things that have influenced us. Hopefully this will also provide some context for the words that we have written in the chapters that follow.

Terry

To start, I would note I am a white, heterosexual man who, at the time of writing, is in his late 40s. I grew up in a working-class family and was within the first generation of my family to go to university. Mental health and well-being were not concepts that were really talked about as I grew up, and the first time I properly encountered psychology as a subject to be studied was during my A-Levels.

> **Positionality** is the recognition that all perspectives, including those of researchers, practitioners, and authors, are shaped by context.

I developed an interest in counselling and therapy whilst in my final year of an undergraduate degree. I completed a unit focusing on counselling skills, and it made me curious to learn more about myself and this type of work with others. Following this, I engaged in care work, youth work, and worked as a school-based counsellor whilst I was training in humanistic integrative counselling. I was then successful in getting funding to complete a research-focused doctorate and worked towards the British Psychological Society's (BPS) Qualification in Counselling Psychology. Once I had completed the latter qualification, I registered as a practitioner psychologist with the Health and Care Professions Council (HCPC) and have since become a Fellow of the BPS. I have been involved in lots of research projects (mainly around the interface between technology and therapy) and have had the pleasure to edit and write/contribute to lots of textbooks focusing on counselling psychology. Alongside my work as an academic, I have also worked therapeutically in a number of settings, with a highlight being running a football therapy group for the organisation Freedom from Torture in Manchester.

Outside of my working role, I live in South Manchester and have a family with three children. I enjoy playing and listening to music and whilst I'm open to most types of music, I generally revert to things with guitars. I worry about the world, would like to live in one that has less poverty and racism, and am generally a little sceptical of those in positions of power. Finally, although the world will always have difficulties to navigate, I am generally quite hopeful. I think these bits of me are partly responsible for my warming to the writings of humanistic psychologists who are interested in the role that humans have to play in this world.

Laura

I've been interested in thinking and talking about people for as long as I can remember: how we feel, how we think, how we interact with others and the world around us. This was likely driven in large part by my own experiences of distress, and the deep impact that the distress of people who were close to me at formative ages had on how I learnt to understand myself and the world.

I benefit from a lot of socially structured advantages, being white, middle-class, cisgender, and heterosexual, and not being currently disabled by my environment. Growing up, I became very interested in inequalities I could see globally and nationally, and when I went to University (to study psychology), talking about and engaging with politics, social structures, and activism became quite normal to me.

But for a long time, I didn't join this interest in society and politics, together with my interest in psychology. Indeed, I was heading down what was (at that time) a fairly 'traditional' pathway for someone who wanted to practice in psychology. My conceptualisation of psychology was heavily individualistic, influenced by the curriculum and readings that were immediately surrounding me. However, over time, and thanks to several key moments with key people, I learned about counselling psychology and its capacity to join my interest in people and my desire to relate to and understand people as individuals, with my interest in the socio-political. I then went on to do some introductory counselling training, followed by a Doctorate in Counselling Psychology at the University of Manchester. And I never really left! I have continued my clinical practice at various times, working with a range of people across the third sector, the National Health Service (NHS), and educational settings, whilst working as a trainer and an academic.

A lot has happened in the last few years of my professional life: in terms of teaching and supervising a huge amount of absolutely amazing human beings who are now qualified (or on the way to being qualified) counselling psychologists; in terms of research and writing; clinical practice; and broader work on equality, diversity, and inclusion at the University. For me, this has all been situated not only in the context of my role as a counselling psychologist, an educator, and an academic but also in my role as a mum – I now have three young children, and it is that which gives me the greatest pleasure, frustration, and learning all at once! Outside of work, I can be found spending time with my family and am most happy in our garden and up on the hills on our doorstep in the Peak District.

How to use this book

There is no single right way to read this book. Some may wish to begin at the start and move through the chapters in sequence. Others may be drawn to particular themes or topics and choose to dip in and out as needed. Each chapter has been designed to stand alone but also contributes to a broader picture of what we see counselling psychology involves.

Reflective activities are included to help you pause, reflect upon the ideas, and consider how they relate to your own thinking, values, or lived experiences. These are not meant to be viewed as assessed tasks, but opportunities to deepen your learning and make the material more personally meaningful.

You may wish to keep a reflective journal as you read, jotting down thoughts, questions, or tensions that arise. Counselling psychology often encourages practitioners to sit with uncertainty, remain open to multiple perspectives, and question their assumptions. The activities in this book aim to support those habits of reflection and curiosity.

Part 1

Key foundations

This section of the book describes what we see to be the key foundations of counselling psychology. We understand foundations to mean the underlying principles upon which counselling psychology rests as a profession and a discipline. The areas we touch upon in this section of the book are viewed as 'load bearing' in the building sense: without these, we think counselling psychology would not hold up.

- In Chapter 1, we look at our origins and purpose, importantly contextualising counselling psychology within the broader history of roles that humans have developed to support others. This understanding situates counselling psychology in a global context and acknowledges both the bigger picture of where we came from as a discipline and the local developments which led to counselling psychology in the UK. We consider our purpose and focus on supporting psychological well-being: emphasising growth and development and understanding common conceptualisations of distress.
- In Chapter 2, we turn to our philosophy, values, and ethics. This covers some core ideas that counselling psychologists might reflect upon as important drivers behind their work, including humanistic, pluralistic and social-justice informed understandings of counselling psychology practice and the wider world.

DOI: 10.4324/9781003546733-2

Chapter 1

Origins and purpose

Introduction

To start, we present our working definition of counselling psychology:

> Counselling psychology is a strand of the applied psychologies that proactively brings together therapeutic and psychological thinking to inform the support that individuals provide to others. Counselling psychologists make use of theory, practice-based learning, research evidence, and personal development activities to make sense of and guide the work that they engage in. This work might take place with individuals, groups, or communities and counselling psychologists might adopt a wide variety of overlapping roles, including being therapists, clinical supervisors, service managers, trainers, researchers, and activists. In all contexts they recognise the importance of being responsive to the unique situations they encounter, embracing the ambiguity inherent in working with humans, and engaging in rich relationships that promote dialogue to help support constructive change.

Whilst this definition could be expanded much further, and we will unpack the different elements further in the chapters of this text that follow, it captures some of the key elements of how counselling psychology is currently defined.

A brief historical perspective

To start, it is important to note that the origins of counselling psychology cannot be attributed to a single event or point in time. The work that counselling psychologists do might be seen on a continuum that reaches back millennia. Throughout the history of humanity, and across

DOI: 10.4324/9781003546733-3

the globe, individuals have taken on roles focused on caring and being empathetic towards others and have been interested in the purpose that humans might have on this earth. These might be religious leaders, mentors, community elders or healers, ancient philosophers, or one of the numerous other roles that might be added to this list. Counselling psychology is certainly not unique in being part of this development but, when considering the history of the applied psychologies, it is important to acknowledge the context from which it has grown. Further, whilst we hope to acknowledge the broader histories of similar roles that individuals have taken up throughout history and across the globe in our writing, we recognise that partly because of who we are as individuals (see Introduction), and partly because of counselling psychology's development in largely, though not exclusively, English speaking countries, that this is limited (see Hanley and Winter (Forthcoming) for a more detailed historical perspective).

Records of psychiatric wards and hospitals supporting individuals experiencing distress go back as far as 705 in Baghdad and the 1280s in Egypt (Awaad et al., 2019; Moodley & van der Tempel, 2018). By the end of the 1800s, and throughout the 1900s, therapeutic practices as they are more commonly understood within contemporary Western society started to be developed. For instance, Bertha Pappenheim's work with her clinician was written up as a case study entitled *Anna O* by Sigmund Freud and Joseph Breuer (Breuer & Freud, 1895). This played a significant role in the development of the conceptualisation of psychoanalysis. At a similar point in history, behaviourism was starting to gather pace as a means of creating behaviour change and as a therapeutic intervention. These theories are discussed in more detail when considering the growth of therapy in Chapter 3, and they also play important roles in the growth of interest in counselling psychology.

Not all psychologists found a natural home in the psychoanalysis and behaviourism camps during the early years of therapy. As a consequence, a group of individuals developed what they classed as a third **force of psychology**, notably humanistic psychology – sometimes also referred to as humanistic-existential (Bugental, 1964). This group included prominent individuals such as Charlotte Bühler, Abraham Maslow, and Carl Rogers, to name but three. At its outset, it was interesting to note that

> **Force of psychology** refers to the major historical movements that have shaped the field of psychology, each introducing distinct perspectives on human behaviour and therapy.

this new force developed under the unifying umbrella of not being either of the other forces in the first instance:

> The *Journal of Humanistic Psychology* is being founded by a group of psychologists and professional men and women from other fields who are interested in those human capacities and potentialities that have no systematic place either in positivistic or behavio[u]ristic theory, or in classical psychoanalytic theory...
>
> (Sutich, 1961, pp. viii–ix)

Despite this oppositional starting point, this swiftly developed into a series of five propositions that articulated the group's position. These emphasised the belief that humans are all unique, have the potential to grow given appropriately fertile environments and have some choice in their lives. They also highlight the close relationship that humans have with the broader natural world.

Alongside the development of humanistic psychology came the growth of counselling. The term was used in the title of Rollo May's book *The Art of Counseling* in 1939, a text focusing upon the development of skills for professionals who engage in counselling activities (May, 1939). Following on from this, Carl Rogers published his developing theory in the book *Counsel[l]ing and Psychotherapy* in 1942 (Rogers, 1942). Both books, whilst dated now, still capture some of the flavour of counselling as offered today. They set the scene for a profession that places great importance upon the relationships between the person seeking support and the supporter. As might be evident, in contrast to the influential European psychoanalysts, many of the initial developments in counselling and humanistic psychology occurred in the United States of America. During this period, individuals, such as Carl Rogers, found themselves at the forefront of providing support and care to individuals returning from the Second World War. Indeed, the initial American Psychological Association Division title in 1946 reflected this, it being *Personnel and Guidance Psychologists* before being changed to *Counselling and Guidance* a few years later. It was ten years later still that it formally became the *Division 17, Counselling Psychology* and more recently still, in 2003, that it changed its name to *The Society of Counselling Psychology* to emphasise its 'unity through diversity'.

During the years in which therapeutic theory started to be utilised within the UK, the work of psychologists separated from the work of counsellors and psychotherapists. Training pathways were created for these latter groups in universities and colleges that were outside of psychology departments. For instance, many counselling courses were situated in departments of education due to the growth of counselling within educational settings (Hanley et al., 2017). Additionally, the British

Association for Counselling (now the **British Association for Counselling and Psychotherapy**) was developed in 1977. Whilst this separation fit for some practitioners, others believed that it underplayed the psychological theory and academic writing that underpinned their therapeutic work. Despite much pushback, these individuals fought for the creation of an official space within the **British Psychological Society** (BPS), the predominant organisation focusing upon psychology within the UK. This eventually led to the development of an interest-based section of Counselling Psychology in the Society in 1982, and a full division of Counselling Psychology in 1994. Counselling Psychology has gone from strength to strength in the UK and, at the time of writing, it is now the second largest division in the BPS.

In 2009, the British Government made the Health Professions Council (HPC), now the **Health and Care Professions Council**

British Association of Counselling and Psychotherapy (BACP) is the professional body that sets standards for counsellors and psychotherapists in the UK, offering accreditation, training, and ethical guidance.

British Psychological Society (BPS) is the professional body representing psychologists in the UK, responsible for promoting excellence in psychology, accrediting courses, and setting ethical and professional standards.

Health and Care Professions Council (HCPC) is the regulatory body that oversees psychologists, arts therapists, and other health and care professionals in the UK, ensuring safe and ethical practice.

Standards of proficiency are a set of minimum professional standards set by the HCPC, detailing the skills, knowledge, and behaviours required for safe and effective practice.

Fitness to practise is the process of assessing whether a practitioner is safe, competent, and ethically able to practise, often in response to complaints, concerns, or breaches of professional standards.

(HCPC), the regulator of the applied psychologies. The HCPC now regulates the work of practitioner psychologists, which is the broader term for the applied psychology divisions, such as clinical, counselling, educational, or forensic psychology. Within this role, the HCPC has developed a series of **Standards of Proficiency** that guide the content of the initial training programmes to become a practitioner psychologist and then monitor ongoing **fitness to practise**. In addition to managing membership and complaints for this group, having a government regulator means that only individuals who have completed relevant training programmes can use the professional titles that they oversee. Thus, unlike titles such as *counsellor, psychologist, psychotherapist,* or *therapist,* titles such as *Counselling Psychologist,* or the more general term *Practitioner Psychologist,* are protected by law, and it would be illegal to work under these titles without being registered with the HCPC.

Despite having its own professional bodies and specific regulation processes, counselling psychology has developed many links and overlaps with work that goes by other names. This includes the work of counsellors, life coaches, therapists (of many specific types), other branches of applied psychology and psychotherapists. Such terms have a wide variety of ways in which they are interpreted, terms that are increasingly aligned to a series of competency statements developed by professional bodies. In many instances, counselling psychologists might offer these activities as part of the work that they do – for instance, they might be a counselling psychologist who offers life coaching, counselling, therapy, or psychotherapy. Some counselling psychologists might specialise in particular approaches, or become consultants in them, whilst others might choose to remain quite broadly focused on the work that they do.

Further afield, counselling psychology also has a major presence. For instance, counselling psychology has significant presence within Australia, Canada, Hong Kong, Ireland, Korea, New Zealand, and South Africa (Orlans & Van Scoyoc, 2009). Additionally, special editions of the International Association of Applied Psychology's journal *Applied Psychology* (published in 2007) and *Counselling Psychology Quarterly* (published in 2016) which focused upon developments in counselling psychology, also included submissions from France, India, Israel, Japan, Portugal, and Taiwan. In recent years, a group entitled the *Global Counselling Psychology Forum* (Global Counselling Psychology Forum, 2024) also added India and Singapore to this list. This group highlights commonalities within the global landscape and helps demonstrate the growing international interest in this division of applied psychology.

The recent history of counselling psychology has been dominated by the contributions of white psychologists based in the Global North. It is therefore important to acknowledge how the profession has often marginalised knowledge systems and voices from racially minoritised communities and the Global South. Forums within professional bodies, such as the BPS's *Black and Asian Counselling Psychologists Group,* have emerged to amplify the contributions of a wider range of psychologists and push the field toward greater inclusivity. Scholars such as Clemont Vontress (see Moodley & Walcott, 2017), Roy Moodley (Moodley & Palmer, 2014), and Pittu Laungani (Laungani, 2007) have long advocated for

> **Geopsychiatry** is a framework that examines how geopolitical, cultural, historical, and environmental forces shape mental health and psychiatric practice across global contexts.

more culturally responsive approaches, urging the profession to question universalist assumptions and embrace a multitude of worldviews. Their work challenges the idea that psychological knowledge is culturally neutral, instead positioning the practice of counselling psychologists as a practice deeply embedded in sociocultural and historical contexts (themes we revisit in later chapters of this text).

Extending these arguments, Castaldelli-Maia and Bhugra (2022) propose **geopsychiatry** as a framework that calls attention to the geopolitical, historical, and environmental dimensions of mental distress. This approach critiques dominant psychiatric and psychological paradigms that ignore the structural conditions, such as colonialism, forced migration, and climate change, that shape people's lives and wellbeing. Geopsychiatry shares counselling psychology's concern with context, power, and ethics, and invites practitioners to consider the global forces that impact mental health, particularly for those historically marginalised. For counselling psychologists, integrating this lens can potentially deepen reflexivity, support social justice work, and challenge siloed or overly individualised models of care. It may also strengthen the profession's commitment to fostering systems of support that are responsive to both individual and collective needs across diverse global settings.

Why do people seek support from a counselling psychologist?

Two questions that we often ask our trainees in the first weeks of university are:

1 What is a human?
2 What makes a good life?

The first is a question that Rollo May opened his 1939 text, referred to above. Whilst it might seem obvious, it is important for people to have a sense of what type of being is sitting in front of them when they seek support and how we personally might make sense of what they share with us. For instance, where do we draw the line of what a human is? (A question that can provoke lots of conversations that are surrounded by contro-versy.) And what makes humans special? (or indeed, are we special?) Following on from this, considering the nature of a 'good life' becomes important for considering what we might be attempting to achieve in therapeutic work. Charlotte Bühler stated:

> I thought, with psychology we should be able to find out how to live life, what we are living for, and how to relate to other persons in life.
>
> (Bühler, 1973, p. 199)

Reflexive activity: what is a good life?

Before continuing, take a minute to consider what you might view as a 'good life'. What might this consist of for you? What do you prioritise when you think of this question? We have listed a few things that you might want to consider below:

Wealth – Health – Happiness – Collective prosperity – Power – Faith – Relationships – Being Accepted – Fame – Being Content – Ethical living

Now, consider which of these elements might be viewed as important within the society that you live in, and how well they match up.

Within the activity above, we would anticipate that you have noted some difference between your personal view and the view that you have attributed to society. Whilst this will differ from person to person and society to society, it is not uncommon that external pressures create dif-ficulties for individuals. Thus, alongside the many challenges individu-als encounter in the world (from births to deaths and everything in between), people are constantly changing. Humans are biopsychosocial beings (Engel, 1978), with our biology, psychology, and society all influ-encing our experiences in the world and the resources that we have to cope with them. Some psychologists also extend this to include extra elements into this description, for instance, O'Brien and Charura refer to bio-psycho-social-sexual-spiritual-existential presentations (O'Brien & Charura, 2024), with each component constantly impacting upon the others. Carl Rogers reflects this fluctuating state in his famous quote:

> The good life is a process, not a state of being. It is a direction, not a destination.
>
> (Rogers, 1961, p. 186)

Given the complex nature of our existence, individuals seek the support of counselling psychologists for an incomprehensibly large number of reasons. As is noted above, humanistic psychologists believe that a person will constructively grow given a fertile environment. This type of support is sometimes referred to as growth-focused or adopting a potentiality model. From this position, individuals are provided with support so that they can learn more about themselves and the situations that they are encountering. This could be events that are commonly experienced negatively such as the death of a loved one, the breakdown of a relationship, being bullied, or overcoming the psychological impact of an accident. It could also focus upon more purposefully growth-focused activities, such as reflecting upon how an individual might complete their job more effectively, understanding their relationship to the broader world that they live in, or working to improve a relationship with a partner. One of the most invigorating things about offering therapy can be the experience of not knowing what you might be working with in your next session. In contrast, being able to tolerate, or indeed embrace the not-knowing in this work, and the ambiguity that can be associated with it, can also be exhausting at times.

Whilst counselling psychologists are heavily influenced by the growth-focused position of humanistic psychology, they also work with what can be framed as the deficit model of support. This is commonplace within healthcare settings in which, historically, the role of medical professionals has been to mend things that are broken (e.g. a doctor will help cure an illness or fix a broken leg). In the context of applied psychology, a medical model perspective often translates to individuals being assessed and, in some instances, receiving a diagnosis – with criteria outlined in a text such as the **Diagnostic and Statistical Manual for Mental Disorders** (the DSM, currently on its fifth edition) or the **International Classification of Diseases** (ICD, currently on its eleventh edition). Often this might be a diagnosis of things like 'Major Depressive Disorder' or 'Generalised Anxiety Disorder' but can spread

Diagnostic and Statistical Manual for Mental Disorders (DSM) is a classification system produced by the American Psychiatric Association, listing and describing mental health disorders along with diagnostic criteria. We are currently on the fifth edition of this Manual.

International Classification of Diseases (ICD) is a global classification system produced by the World Health Organization, covering all diseases and health conditions, including mental and behavioural disorders. We are currently on the eleventh edition of this Manual.

the full spectrum of diagnostic categories. It is certainly not uncommon for counselling psychologists to meet with people with diagnoses of difficulties such as eating disorders, post-traumatic stress disorder, or psychosis. There are many critiques of these categories that have been articulated (e.g. Pilgrim, 2014); however, it is important that counselling psychologists are familiar with the lists of symptoms and the various therapeutic approaches that are strongly indicated to be most beneficial with them. Whilst these evidence-based approaches will not be appropriate for everyone with the same diagnosis, any variation must be made in an informed way. It is therefore not uncommon for counselling psychologists to view specific diagnoses as societal constructs that need to be understood in more detail, rather than simplistically understood facts that are not open to scrutiny.

Due to the complexity of the issues, difficulties, or indeed illnesses that people want to work with in the therapy room, the work of counselling psychologists might take numerous forms. There is no one-size-fits-all approach for the work that they engage in, and a counselling psychologist must be creative and responsive to the wants and needs of the individuals seeking support. This might include providing psychoeducational support, therapy, crisis support or taking on the role of an advocate. They might also work with individuals and groups of people or attempt to make changes to systems. Importantly, however, in whatever context they work, counselling psychologists make sense of their work using psychological theory. For example, they might view their therapy through a cognitive-behavioural or person-centred lens, or they might justify their activist work with a psychodynamic understanding of abuses of power (approaches discussed in more depth later in this text). This psychological underpinning is important to both make sense of what people want to work on with the psychologist, thus guiding the way that they may provide support in the most informed way as possible, and provide a robust support to practitioners, who are often attempting to navigate relatively murky waters.

Training to be a counselling psychologist

Training to be a counselling psychologist is a challenging pursuit. Within the UK, in addition to usual academic studies which focus upon individuals learning about theory and conducting research, trainees have to offer a substantial amount of therapeutic work in placement settings and engage in personal development activities. The training usually takes place on a Doctorate in Counselling Psychology programme, which is approved by the HCPC and has further accreditation with the BPS – these organisations provide up-to-date lists of relevant providers on their websites noted in the resources section. The BPS has also provided a portfolio-based route to qualification for people with existing backgrounds in psychology and therapy.

Whilst individual institutions have their own entry criteria, prior to studying for a Counselling Psychology qualification, individuals typically need to have:

- A psychology undergraduate degree – that provides Graduate Basis for Chartered (GBC) status with the BPS, grounds people in both psychological theory, and gives them some experience of conducting a research project
- Some previous counselling training – for example, a certificate in counselling (usually a one-year part-time programme in which people engage in in-person training activities)
- Relevant experience in therapeutic or supportive roles – such as voluntary work with mental health charities, helplines, youth services, or care settings, which helps applicants gain insight into relational work and the realities of supporting others
- A personal readiness to work as a counselling psychologist – this relates to people's ability to reflect on their experiences, their maturity, and robustness for engaging in this type of challenging work
- Satisfactory criminal records checks

Each organisation has slightly different processes and priorities for assessing the above, but it would be usual that a prospective student would have to both provide a written application (which might include developing a personal statement, a research proposal and providing evidence of previous studies) and take part in an interview process (which might include answering a series of questions, engaging in a role play activity or completing a presentation). Unlike some applied psychology training programmes, counselling psychology is predominantly self-funded, with only relatively few exceptions to this nationally. The application process therefore provides an important opportunity for the institutions to assess candidates and for candidates to assess institutions.

Once on a counselling psychology programme, trainees will take part in a rich diet of activities. These will include class-based activities that will introduce individuals to several therapeutic approaches (at least two different models) and require them to demonstrate specific therapeutic skills in assessment activities. Programmes also introduce individuals to a wide array of research skills, ultimately supporting them to complete a piece of original research around a relevant topic. Two vitally important components, that are often not required within earlier levels of study, are that trainees have to complete several placements where they offer a substantial number of supervised therapeutic hours as a trainee counselling psychologist (usually 450 hours) and that they also have to be in therapy themselves for typically at least 40 hours during the time they are completing their studies – being in the role of client and experiencing what it is like to seek out a therapist, sit in the waiting room and everything that follows is an incredibly important learning experience.

The placements that people attend vary greatly and are often constructed around the trainees' hopes for the future. They might include work in the National Health Service (NHS), educational settings (e.g. schools or universities), forensic settings (e.g. prisons or centres supporting young offenders), third sector organisations (e.g. bereavement services, support for those seeking refuge or survivors of abuse or torture), or working in private healthcare settings. Further, this work might involve working with individuals, those in relationships or larger groups, and take place in-person or in a mediated format (e.g. online or via the telephone). Consequently, trainees who complete these programmes end up being very experienced practitioners as they enter their new roles as fully qualified counselling psychologists. This also means that graduates are eligible to apply for jobs in all these settings, and it is not uncommon that a counselling psychology graduate is successful in obtaining a job that has been advertised as a practitioner psychologist, counsellor, or psychotherapist.

The many roles of a counselling psychologist

Once an individual has qualified as a counselling psychologist, a wide variety of potential roles become available to them. For instance, a counselling psychologist might become:

- A therapist offering counselling or psychotherapy in independent practice, healthcare, education, or community settings
- A lecturer or trainer working in higher education, delivering continuing professional development, or shaping future generations of psychologists
- A service manager or team leader with responsibility for overseeing clinical teams and developing psychologically informed services
- A clinical supervisor supporting other practitioners in reflective practice, ethical development, and clinical decision-making
- An advocate for individuals, groups, or systemic changes to enhance access, equity, and inclusion in mental health provision
- An activist engaging in work that challenges structural inequalities and promotes social justice within and beyond psychological services
- A service commissioner involved in shaping, funding, and designing psychological services at organisational or regional levels

- A researcher generating evidence, shaping theory, and evaluating innovative practices to improve outcomes
- A consultant bringing psychological expertise to other professions or sectors (e.g. schools, charities, businesses, or policy organisations)
- A writer or communicator who translates psychological ideas for wider audiences through books, blogs, podcasts, or public engagement work

Many counselling psychologists move fluidly between these roles, often combining clinical work with teaching, research, supervision, or service development throughout their careers. What makes these roles distinct within counselling psychology is the philosophical grounding of the profession (see Chapter 2 for an overview of this). Counselling psychologists are trained not only to work with psychological distress but also to consider the wider systemic, cultural, and social factors that shape people's lives. This means that whether they are offering therapy, managing services, or engaging in research or advocacy, counselling psychologists bring a critically reflective, research-informed, humanistic perspective that challenges one-size-fits-all approaches and promotes collaborative, ethically grounded practice.

Conclusion

This chapter outlines how counselling psychology might be seen as being one of a range of helping professions which stretches back millennia. It highlights that, whilst informed by all the original 'forces' of psychology, it has been heavily influenced by developments in humanistic psychology and notes how this has acted as a catalyst for counselling psychology to grow in the UK and beyond. Following on from this, we go on to consider how incredibly complex humans are and that those who seek support do so for a wide array of reasons. Counselling psychologists value a perspective that emphasises the potential for growth and are also informed by the concepts from the medical model, such as diagnosis. Psychological theory therefore helps to both challenge and make sense of the support they are providing. Finally, the multifaceted training pathways for counselling psychology are briefly described, before ending by outlining some of the many roles that trained counselling psychologists might adopt.

Reflexive questions

1   How might it be for you listening to someone who is in distress? Maybe they have been recently bereaved, are worried about being bullied at school or work, or have been told they only have six months to live.
2   Imagine a situation when you have been upset with yourself. If you reflect upon this, what did you want from other people?

Critical thinking questions

1 Why might creating divisions between the applied psychologies (e.g. clinical, counselling, educational, forensic psychology or occupational psychology) be helpful?
2 Why might these divisions be unhelpful?

Further reading and resources

- **BPS website – https://www.bps.org.uk/**
  This is the website for the British Psychological Society. This includes a specific area for the Division of Counselling Psychology (DCoP).
- **HCPC website – https://www.hcpc-uk.org/**
  This is the website for the regulatory body that oversees practitioner psychologists in the UK. It includes links to the standards of proficiency expected for all counselling psychologists.
- **Global Counselling Psychology position statement – https://counselling-psychology-position-paper.tiiny.site/**
  This statement provides a unified international perspective on counselling psychology.

References

Awaad, R., Mohammad, A., Elzamzamy, K., Fereydooni, S., & Gamar, M. (2019). Mental health in the Islamic golden era: The historical roots of modern psychiatry. In H. S. Moffic, J. Peteet, A. Z. Hankir, & R. Awaad (Eds.), *Islamophobia and psychiatry: Recognition, prevention, and treatment* (pp. 3–17). Springer International Publishing. https://doi.org/10.1007/978-3-030-00512-2_1

Breuer, J., & Freud, S. (1895). *Studien über Hysterie [Studies on hysteria]*. F. Deuticke.

Bugental, J. F. T. (1964). The third force in psychology. *Journal of Humanistic Psychology, 4*(1), 19–26. https://doi.org/10.1177/002216786400400102

Bühler, C. (1973). Humanistic psychology as a personal experience. *Interpersonal Development, 4*(4), 197–214.

Castaldelli-Maia, J. M., & Bhugra, D. (2022). What is geopsychiatry? *International Review of Psychiatry, 34*(1), 1–2. https://doi.org/10.1080/09540261.2022.2031915

Engel, G. L. (1978). The Biopsychosocial model and the education of health professionals. *Annals of the New York Academy of Sciences, 310*(1), 169–181. https://doi.org/10.1111/j.1749-6632.1978.tb22070.x

Global Counselling Psychology Forum. (2024). *Counselling psychology—Position paper*. https://counselling-psychology-position-paper.tiiny.site/

Hanley, T., Noble, J., & Toor, N. (2017). Policy, policy research on school-based counselling in the United Kingdom. In *International handbook for policy research on school-based counseling* (pp. 353–364). Springer International Publishing/Springer Nature. https://doi.org/10.1007/978-3-319-58179-8_23

Hanley, T., & Winter, L. A. (Forthcoming). Historical context of psychological therapies. In C. O'Brien & D. Charura (Eds.), *Counselling psychology and psychotherapy training*. PCCS Books Ltd.

Laungani, P. D. (2007). *Understanding cross-cultural psychology: Eastern and western perspectives*. Sage Publications Ltd.

May, R. (1939). *The art of counseling*. Abingdon Press.

Moodley, R., & Palmer, S. (2014). *Race, Culture and psychotherapy: Critical perspectives in multicultural practice*. Routledge.

Moodley, R., & van der Tempel, J. (2018). Contexts, epistemologies and practices of global south psychologies. In S. Fernando & R. Moodley (Eds.), *Global psychologies: Mental health and the global south* (pp. 59–74). Palgrave Macmillan UK. https://doi.org/10.1057/978-1-349-95816-0_4

Moodley, R., & Walcott, R. (2017). *Counseling across and beyond cultures: Exploring the work of Clemmont E. Vontress in clinical practice*. University of Toronto Press.

O'Brien, C., & Charura, D. (2024). Body mapping refugees and asylum seekers' perspectives of embodied trauma: An innovative method for psychotraumatology research & practice. *Qualitative Research in Psychology*, *21*(1), 71–106. https://doi.org/10.1080/14780887.2023.2289964

Orlans, V., & Van Scoyoc, S. (2009). *A short introduction to counselling psychology*. Sage.

Pilgrim, D. (2014). *Understanding mental health: A critical realist exploration*. Routledge.

Rogers, C. R. (1942). *Counseling and psychotherapy: Newer concepts in practice*. Houghton Mifflin.

Rogers, C. R. (1961). *On becoming a person: A therapist's view of psychotherapy*. Houghton Mifflin.

Sutich, A. J. (1961). Introduction. *Journal of Humanistic Psychology*, *1*(1), vii–ix. https://doi.org/10.1177/002216786100100101

Chapter 2

Philosophy, values, and ethics

Introduction

Though individual practitioners will vary in their own personal values, ethics, and principles, and what counselling psychology practice looks like varies from individual to individual, much has been written about the shared principles underlying the discipline. Given the range of different ways of working and practices within counselling psychology, it seems understandable that people might ask, *what unites the profession? What underpins the work that we do, even if it does look different and happens across a wide range of different settings and frameworks?* This chapter looks at these questions and focuses on the values, philosophies, and ethics that have been said to unite the discipline and give counselling psychology its flavour. When we say 'philosophy, values, and ethics', we are referring to the ideas we have about what is 'right', what we think is important, and how we understand the world we work in and the people we work with.

Some might say that the things discussed in this chapter make counselling psychology 'unique'. You'll note that we don't say this. Partly this is because it is almost impossible to make such broad generalisations about professions, when of course professions are made up of individuals, and they shift over time depending on developments and changes. But beyond just this, it is because of the dangers of thinking in these 'us and them' terms (counselling psychology vs. clinical psychology or counselling psychology vs. psychotherapy, for example). This can be divisive and is potentially not aligned with the values we discuss! So, the values, philosophy, and ethics described here might not be what makes counselling psychology entirely unique, and not all counselling psychologists will agree entirely with everything presented. But, broadly speaking across the profession, they are viewed as important and, we argue, these values and philosophies drive much of the work of practitioners, researchers, and trainers in the field. As such, they might be seen as permeating through our thinking and our practice. However, values are nothing without action, so what is presented here should be seen as the beginning, rather

DOI: 10.4324/9781003546733-4

than the end. Articulated values can become empty, meaningless, and only function as buzzwords that allow us to "...believe change is happening" (Wilcox et al., 2024, p. 7). This chapter lays the groundwork for the rest of this book, where these values must come to life in our counselling psychology practice, to create real change.

Humanistic psychology

Most introductions to counselling psychology emphasise the humanistic underpinnings of the profession, as we did in Chapter 1. Indeed, the BPS says that counselling psychology in the UK "holds a humanistic value base" (2019, p. 6) and a recent position paper on global counselling psychology notes that counselling psychology is grounded in a 'humanistic perspective' (Global Counselling Psychology Forum, 2024, p. 16). The 'humanistic' in these values and perspectives can often be mistaken, and sometimes people think that it means that all counselling psychologists use humanistic therapeutic models in all their practice, such as only using person-centred counselling (Rogers, 1951). Instead, the humanistic base that people refer to relates more to the assumptions which underpin practice, and the views of what a person is. It's not about a model for practice, or what we do (in fact, not all counselling psychologists will be trained in a humanistic therapeutic model). Counselling psychology is grounded in values which stem from **humanistic psychology**, which does not mean that all counselling psychology therapeutic practice adopts one of the often-described humanistic therapies.

Humanistic psychology centres on understanding a person as someone who can constructively grow (i.e. to flourish and work towards reaching their potential as humans), given the right circumstances. For example, Rogers talked about the 'actualising tendency'. This growth-orientation does not deny that people feel distressed or struggle to make positive change, and the tendency itself focuses on growth rather than just positive growth per se. Instead, it means we understand people as, in principle, being able to make the change required to feel well, *if they are in the right environment*. This right environment is typically thought of as being where others are accepting, where they are understanding and genuine, and where we can

Humanistic psychology is a theoretical approach that understands a person as someone who is unique, more than the sum of their parts, and who can constructively grow (i.e. to flourish and work towards reaching their potential as humans), given the right circumstances.

connect with and experience this. People are seen as having capacity and agency. Humanistic psychology also understands people as irreducible to a single story or part of themselves. The often-cited phrase 'the whole is greater than the sum of its parts' captures this idea of a holistic approach. This doesn't mean that having a label for things (such as a diagnosis) is always a completely bad idea. Nor does it mean that all counselling psychologists always fundamentally disagree with people having mental health diagnoses. But it does mean that we don't think we can fully understand the person solely through understanding a diagnosis they may have been given. They are more than that, and they are unique. Finally, humanistic psychological perspectives understand the person as making meaning. This individual meaning-making and construction of our own worlds is important for how a person feels and thinks. The relational emphasis of these humanistic psychology values guides our thinking, for example, on professional ethics. Counselling psychologists, rooted in this relational stance, emphasise the importance of compassionate and genuine relationships in all that we do. Therefore, ethical thinking and decision-making needs to go beyond ethical codes published by professional bodies (Finlay, 2019).

The connections between humanistic psychology and counselling psychology have been made explicit in Cooper's (2009) six key principles of counselling psychology. These are as follows:

1   A prioritisation of the client's subjective, and intersubjective, experiencing (vs. a prioritisation of the therapist's observations, or 'objective' measures).
2   A focus on facilitating growth and the actualisation of potential (vs. a focus on treating pathology).
3   An orientation towards empowering clients (vs. viewing empowerment as an adjunct to an absence of mental illness).
4   A commitment to a democratic non-hierarchical relationship (vs. a stance of therapist-as-expert.
5   An appreciation of the client as a unique being (vs. viewing the client as an instance of universal laws).
6   An understanding of the client as a socially and relationally embedded being, including an awareness that the client may be experiencing discrimination and prejudice (vs. a wholly intra-psychic focus).

These are united by the idea that counselling psychologists commit to view the people they work with as 'agentic human subjectivities who cannot be reduced to, or treated as, objects of natural scientific enquiry'. Cooper's inclusion of the individual being socially embedded highlights another element of the humanistic psychology perspective. Humanistic perspectives have been criticised for their insufficient attention to the environment, and the lack of emphasis on the political nature of distress. But others have highlighted humanistic psychology's potentially radical view of people and how this differs from other branches of psychology. Humanistic psychology increasingly understands people as embedded in ecological systems and therefore sees social justice and politics as relevant to well-being, though traditional humanistic psychology theory did not always emphasise this.

In short, the humanistic philosophy and value base of counselling psychology is about an ethics of practice where we treat other people as:

- Unique
- Being able to make their own decisions
- Able to grow and develop
- Inseparable from social and political systems
- Unable to be broken down and understood in parts

Whilst different counselling psychologists, using different approaches to their work, might translate these values into practice in their own ways, they are said to underpin everything that we do.

Reflexive activity: considering how humans grow

Carl Rogers' potato analogy is a great illustration of the humanistic idea of our tendency towards growth:

> Imagine you leave an old potato at the back of your cupboard. When you find it a long time later, it's sprouted little white nubs which are directed towards any crack of light around the door to the cupboard. He argues that this shows how organisms grow and develop even in unfavourable conditions.

What do you think about the idea that human beings have an inherent tendency to grow and develop?

A pluralistic perspective

It is also often said that counselling psychology is 'pluralistic' in nature. This philosophy means that 'no one size fits all'. In short, because individuals are unique, they generate their own understandings of the world; they have their own knowledge and understanding of themselves, so we can't say that one thing will always help. This stands in contrast with views that we can know what is right for our clients, based on their list of symptoms or diagnosis, and we can (as the expert counselling psychologist) direct the correct route to psychological well-being. Our pluralistic philosophical roots mean that, instead, we prize the uniqueness of individuals' own wants and needs and place an emphasis on dialogue with people to jointly direct the course of our work together. As with

> **Pluralistic philosophy** is a view that 'no one size fits all', and that there will be multiple valid answers to the same questions.

our discussions on the humanistic underpinnings of the discipline we talked about earlier, adopting a **pluralistic philosophy** is not to be confused with adopting a pluralistic framework (Cooper & McLeod, 2011) approach to all our therapeutic interactions and work as a counselling psychologist.

For counselling psychologists, being grounded in this pluralistic understanding typically translates to an understanding that a variety of ways of working can be helpful. Counselling psychologists train in multiple models of and approaches to working with people, and though particular individuals undoubtedly have their preferences and models which they use more often with clients, the pluralistic philosophical underpinnings tend to mean that they are open to using different approaches with different people and at different times. So rather than saying that your client has depression and therefore you'll use cognitive-behaviour therapy because it's a recommended way of working (e.g. by the National Institute for Health and Care Excellence (NICE)), counselling psychologists are likely to try to understand what this particular client's experience is like, what their preferences for therapy are, and potentially use cognitive-behaviour therapy and/or potentially use other approaches or methods too. A pluralistic attitude will mean remaining open to other ways of understanding things and other ways of working, even when only choosing to use a single model with a particular client. It means adopting an understanding that all the client's knowledge and our various sources of knowledge are important. It is not only knowledge from large-scale controlled research trials that can inform us how to practice. Our personal experiences (inside and outside of psychological work), our connection with our culture(s) and histories, the natural world, and a multitude of other things can also be considered as important sources of knowledge within a pluralistic way of working. When asked about what influences therapeutic work most, many therapists note their previous work with clients or discussions with clinical supervisors as hugely influential (Orlinsky et al., 2001). This openness to different ways of working, and bringing different models together, is not without risks, however, for example, there can be tensions in how we reconcile different views of people and theories of distress. It's important for counselling psychologists to be *truly* open also and to consider which ways of knowing or sources of knowledge are often neglected (see 'epistemic justice' in Chapter 10).

The pluralistic philosophy adopted by counselling psychologists also often refers to engaging in open and transparent dialogue and communication with our clients about their needs and preferences for therapy (Smith & de la Prida, 2021). Collaboration and shared decision-making are important positions and moving away from an expert psychologist role. Counselling psychologists may emphasise the importance of meta-communication, meaning communicating with clients about our communication. For example, we can check-in with clients about how they are finding sessions, how they felt when we said something, as well as sharing how we feel or what we think when they say something. As might be evident from the discussion above, dialogue and genuine communication with those counselling psychologists engage with are vitally important in our work.

Social justice and anti-oppressive practice

Counselling psychologists also take a socially and politically embedded approach. We are guided by values of equality, fairness, and 'social justice'. **Social justice** has been cited as a core value of the profession globally. It is a somewhat tricky term to define, but it broadly relates to things like equality, anti-oppressive practices, fairness, inclusion, and shared decision-making (Winter & Charura, 2023). Counselling psychology therefore does not aim to be value-free, apolitical, or neutral. When we refer to 'political', however, we aren't talking necessarily about electoral politics, and you shouldn't expect a counselling psychologist will be telling you who to vote for in elections. But it does mean that we acknowledge that the work we do occurs in a political context and that our work can have political implications, when you think about politics as also about power in society.

Research shows us that our well-being and mental health are significantly impacted by a multitude of social, economic, and political factors. For example, global crises such as pandemics and wars, displacement of peoples and communities, structural discrimination and oppression such as racism, sexism, and other 'isms', all have been shown to impact us negatively. Counselling psychologists adopt a critical psychology perspective which acknowledges this and sees individuals as embedded in and inseparable from these systems, as we discuss further in Chapter 4.

Humanistic psychology has been critiqued for its colonial, white, male-dominated theory. Ideas such as the actualising tendency from Rogerian theory are formulated in such a way in the theoretical literature

> **Social justice** is both a goal and a process which broadly relates to things like equality, anti-oppressive practices, fairness, inclusion, and shared decision-making.

because of the historical, social, and political context in which Rogers and other core authors were situated. Undoubtedly, one could work in a way which is humanistic but not social justice informed, or pluralistic but not social justice informed. Despite this, we think that social justice can connect well with the values and philosophies of both humanistic psychology and pluralism described so far (acknowledging though that there are some areas of disagreement and misalignment). For example, the social justice values underpinning counselling psychology and the commitment to equality (which is relational as well as resource-based – we discuss this further in Chapter 4) mean that we centre the voice and experience of the person we are working with. Humanistic psychology, pluralism, and social justice perspectives are all in agreement that dialogue, collaboration, and shared decision-making are all ethically important. Research also shows that collaboration can improve outcomes; however, from a social justice perspective, this is a principles-based, value-driven ethical decision.

Adopting a critical psychology, social justice approach means being critical of everything *including of counselling psychology as a discipline*. It is important to acknowledge the damage that psychology has done and continues to do, and the ways in which counselling psychologists are complicit in (and take an active role in) oppressive systems. But this does not mean that we can't try to work to change those systems for the better. Critical psychology and community psychology approaches are both relevant to counselling psychology practice, and their values and ethics encourage us to understand the power that counselling psychology (and individual counselling psychologists) hold. An understanding of power and the influence of power in society and our lives is important and relevant to counselling psychology's roots in humanistic psychology, pluralism, and social justice. We can think about power in many ways, and it is important to remember that power is relational and influences the relationships between individuals, groups, and communities. Our individual and group history, our social identity, our role in society, and more, all influence the way in which power influences people. For example, a counselling psychologist working with a client has some power because of their role and authority as a highly trained healthcare professional. They might also have different power relationships due to their social identities and positionality, for example, because of their racialised identity, their gender, or their age. We talk more about intersectionality and how this relates to power and society in Chapter 4.

The reflective-practitioner, the scientist-practitioner, and the scientist-practitioner-advocate models

An important thread running through everything we have talked about so far in this chapter is reflective practice and reflexivity. Humanistic psychology, pluralism, and social justice all emphasise reflexivity, as does counselling psychology as a discipline. Reflective practice involves a counselling psychologist considering (reflecting) on their experience to inform their ongoing development and growth as a practitioner. Reflection involves observing your own assumptions, thoughts, feelings, responses, and reactions to a situation or an interaction, considering how these impacted your practice and how others (e.g. clients or colleagues) may have experienced or been impacted by your behaviour. Reflection can occur either in the moment (reflection-in-action) or after an event (reflection-on-action).

Counselling psychologists think that this reflexive process contributes to improving our practice and our reflection can inform our decision-making. Because of how important we consider reflection and the reflexive process to be, counselling psychologists engage in lots of different activities to try and enhance this process. For example, during training students are required to have their own personal therapy, where they bring their own experiences as a client to grow and develop, and to learn about themselves as well as the therapeutic process. We also have supervision for our clinical work, where you talk to an experienced colleague about the work you are doing, how you are experiencing it, how it is going, and how it could be improved. Many practitioners also keep journals, have additional peer supervision, or use other creative methods to engage in reflexive practice.

The **reflective-practitioner model** is an important underpinning for counselling psychology. The humanistic, pluralistic, and social justice philosophies and values described above all involve a considerable amount of reflexivity. The relational approach in humanistic psychology means that the person of the therapist becomes important: who I am as a counselling psychologist will influence my relationships with my clients. And if my relationships are (at least part of) the thing that helps someone grow or change, then I need to look at myself as well as the other person. For example, if I am to be non-judgemental and genuine, I need to honestly reflect on my assumptions, preconceptions, and biases about the world and about people. Social justice approaches encourage us to remember that this reflexivity must include reflection on my social and political identities and how those impact the relationships I build as a counselling psychologist. As noted in Chapter 1, when in training counselling psychologists are required to engage in their own personal therapy, and many qualified practitioners continue to make use of this to manage the emotional nature of the work

> **Reflective-practitioner model** is an understanding that counselling psychology training and practice should emphasise the way in which ongoing reflection on and reflection in action contributes to our work.

we are involved in. Simi-
larly, clinical supervision
and reflexive journaling
or other activities sup-
port our ongoing reflex-
ive development.

> **Scientist-practitioner model** is an
> understanding that counselling psy-
> chology training and practice should
> integrate both research evidence and
> clinical practice, with both informing
> the other.

Alongside this emp-
hasis on reflexivity, counselling   psychologists
are also informed by
research evidence and make use of the **scientist-practitioner model**. The
scientist-practitioner model emphasises the integration of research ('science') and practice. As referred to in the previous chapter, to train as a
counselling psychologist in the UK you need to complete a doctoral-level
qualification, which typically involves conducting an original piece of
doctoral-level research and training in a range of research methods and
approaches. Counselling psychologists take their knowledge and understanding of research and 'evidence' and bring this into their clinical practice. For example, a counselling psychologist may be informed by the
NICE guidelines which are developed based on evidence from randomised-
controlled trials of therapeutic practice for specific diagnoses. Or they might
be informed by recent developments in research in a particular area, which
they learn about at some continuing professional development training.
Research is then also informed by clinical practice. For example, a counselling psychologist might have conducted work with trauma presentations
for several years as a practitioner and have developed some ideas about
what works and what doesn't work. They might then apply for some funding to investigate this further in a piece of empirical work. One of the
main questions surrounding the scientist-practitioner model in counselling psychology is what counts as 'research' (or 'science'). For example,
do we only need to know about randomised-controlled trial evidence, or
systematic reviews and meta-analyses of large-scale quantitative studies? Or
is it also useful to be informed by the findings of qualitative case studies,
or practice-based evidence from small-scale non-controlled or randomised
studies? As a discipline counselling psychology tends towards valuing methodological pluralism in research (which we come back to in Chapter 7) and
therefore values a multitude of approaches and sources of evidence.

Importantly, drawing on both the reflective-practitioner model and the
scientist-practitioner models means being informed by a wide range of pieces
of information, including for example being open to learning from the clients and individuals we work with (experts by experience), learning from
our own experiences, learning from research, and learning from previous
practice. More recently, given the increasing emphasis on social justice and
advocacy (supporting or standing up for the rights, experiences, and views

of others who tend to be marginalised), a **scientist-practitioner-advocate model** has been outlined (Mallinckrodt et al., 2014). This suggests that the role of a psychologist as an advocate, and the way in which advocacy might complement and develop psychologists' practitioner and scientist roles, are important in training and practice. Therefore, drawing together the social justice and anti-oppressive values described above with our emphasis on both the reflective-practitioner and scientist-practitioner models, with more recent work on advocacy and social justice, the work of counselling psychologists might be said to be underpinned by a *reflective-scientist-practitioner-advocate model*.

Reflective-scientist-practitioner-advocate model is an understanding that counselling psychology training and practice should emphasise the importance of ongoing reflection on and in action, research evidence, and advocacy skills. Further, all these areas of influence and work should interact and inform one another.

Scientist-practitioner-advocate model is an understanding that counselling psychology training and practice should not only integrate clinical practice and research evidence knowledge and skills but also incorporate how we advocate for the needs of marginalised groups in our work.

Conclusion

In this chapter, we have introduced you to some of the core guiding philosophies, values, and ethics that underpin the work of counselling psychologists across various settings and in the various models they work within. We suggest that counselling psychologists are guided by a humanistic psychology commitment to relationships, which nurture growth, agency, and individuality; by a pluralistic understanding that no one size fits all and that dialogue and collaboration are important in our work; and by social justice and anti-oppressive practices, which encourage us to look at the social and political context of our work and to challenge inequality and discrimination within our roles. We unpack the reflective-scientist-practitioner-advocate model, which underpins the work of counselling psychologists.

Reflexive questions

1 What are some of your own core values and ethics? How do you think that these influence your work, or will influence your work, as a counselling psychologist?

2 Think about a time when you've experienced a really unequal relationship (maybe with a colleague, teacher, friend, or family member). What did this feel like and how did it impact you? How about a time when you've experienced a really equal relationship?

Critical thinking questions

1 Do you think that all people, given the right environment, can grow and develop?
2 A pluralistic position suggests that there are many different options that can be taken in response to a single question. How do you think different therapeutic approaches compare, and are some more valid than others?

Further reading and resources

- **Milton, M. (Ed.),** *Therapy and beyond: Counselling psychology contributions to therapeutic and social issues.* **Wiley.**
  This edited collection provides a useful overview of counselling psychology which delves into some of the values and philosophies discussed here.
- **The Global Counselling Psychology position statement – https:// counselling-psychology-position-paper.tiiny.site/**
  This recent position statement has relevant sections on values and philosophies underpinning the profession across the world.

References

BPS. (2019). *Standards for the accreditation of doctoral programmes in counselling psychology.* BPS.

Cooper, M. (2009). Welcoming the other: Actualising the humanistic ethic at the core of counselling psychology practice. *Counselling Psychology Review, 24*(3–4), 119–129.

Cooper, M., & McLeod, J. (2011). *Pluralistic counselling and psychotherapy.* Sage.

Finlay, L. (2019). *Practical ethics in counselling and psychotherapy: A relational approach.* Sage.

Global Counselling Psychology Forum. (2024). *Counselling psychology—Position paper.* https://counselling-psychology-position-paper.tiiny.site/

Mallinckrodt, B., Miles, J. R., & Levy, J. J. (2014). The scientist-practitioner-advocate model: Addressing contemporary training needs for social justice advocacy. *Training and Education in Professional Psychology, 8*(4), 303–311. https://doi.org/10.1037/tep0000045

Orlinsky, D. E., Botermans, J. F., & Rønnestad, M. H. (2001). Towards an empirically grounded model of psychotherapy training: Four thousand therapists rate influences on their development. *Australian Psychologist, 36*(2), 139–148. https://doi.org/10.1080/00050060108259646

Rogers, C. R. (1951). *Client-centered therapy: Its current practice, implications and theory.* Robinson.

Smith, K., & de la Prida, A. (2021). *The pluralistic therapy primer: A concise introduction.* PCCS Books.

Wilcox, M. M., Pérez-Rojas, A. E., Marks, L. R., Reynolds, A. L., Suh, H. N., Flores, L. Y., McCubbin, L. D., Wilkins-Yel, K. G., & Miller, M. J. (2024). Structural competencies: Re-Grounding counseling psychology in antiracist and decolonial praxis. *The Counseling Psychologist, 52*(4), 650–691. https://doi.org/10.1177/00110000241231029

Winter, L. A., & Charura, D. (2023). An introduction to the handbook of social justice in psychological therapies. In L. A. Winter & D. Charura (Eds.), *The handbook of social justice in psychological therapies: Power, politics, change* (pp. 3–9). Sage.

Part 2

Key theories

This section of the book takes a closer look at some key theories in counselling psychology. We understand theory as one lens through which counselling psychologists might make sense of their practice and work. We divide this into three core areas of how counselling psychologists might think about what they do: thinking about therapy, thinking about systems, and thinking about leadership. This division does not suggest that the theoretical ideas presented in Chapter 3 cannot be applied to one's leadership practice, but instead that we may draw upon different levels of theory at different times.

- In Chapter 3, we focus on how counselling psychologists may think about the therapeutic work they are engaged in. We introduce three dominant 'forces' in the world of psychology, psychoanalysis/psychodynamic, behaviourism/cognitive and humanistic-existential approaches, and consider how these might be combined into integrative therapeutic approaches. Following on from this, we consider two 'dimensions' that pervade all therapeutic work, namely the transcultural and social justice dimensions.
- In Chapter 4, we start to consider the various systems that counselling psychologists understand and work within. More specifically, we consider how counselling psychologists ensure that the work we do does not ignore the contexts and environments within which we, and the people we work with (clients and colleagues), are embedded in.
- In Chapter 5, we introduce the ways in which counselling psychologists might think about and engage in leadership practices: in both specifically designated managerial roles within services or areas (which they might progress into after a number of years following qualification) and many other roles or practices which involve influencing an area of work or disrupting typical practices. We see the way in which counselling psychologists might disrupt, influence, and lead in a multitude of ways that are consistent with their foundations introduced in Part 1.

DOI: 10.4324/9781003546733-5

Chapter 3

Thinking about therapy

Introduction

One of the most common activities that counselling psychologists engage in as part of their psychological practice is therapy. For ease, and to reflect the view that many therapeutic approaches have more similarities than they have differences, we will refer to the term *therapy* as an umbrella for activities that might also be called *counselling* or *psychotherapy*. The term therapy can be traced back to the Greek word θεραπεία, which refers to the act of healing or care. The related adjective therapeutic, derived from θεραπευτικός (therapeutikós), describes something that promotes healing. Both terms originate from the Greek verb θεραπεύω (therapeúo), meaning to care for or to serve. With these definitions in mind, therapists might therefore be understood as those who attend to others with the purpose of facilitating healing or alleviating suffering. When placed into a broader context, a fuller definition might be:

> Counselling and psychotherapy are mainly, though not exclusively, listening-and-talking-based methods of addressing psychological and sometimes psychosomatic problems, including deep and prolonged human suffering, situational dilemmas, crises and developmental needs, and aspirations towards the realization of human potential. In contrast to biomedical approaches, the psychological therapies operate largely without medication or other physical interventions and may be concerned not only with mental health but with spiritual, philosophical, social and other aspects of living.
>
> (Hanley, 2023, p. 2)

As is evident from this definition, therapeutic work can encompass a very broad remit. It can focus upon supporting people in distress, aid those who want their lives to flourish, and everything that might combine elements of both to varying degrees. Further, it is important to note that therapy never occurs in a vacuum. Therapy commonly takes the form of

DOI: 10.4324/9781003546733-6

meetings with a therapist for a limited period, typically 50 minutes per week. It is therefore quite a fleeting part of a person's life and by no means a panacea for all the world's ills. Outside of this contact, individuals go back to the worlds in which they may be struggling to feel at home in the cultures, families, friendship groups, etc., that they inhabit and often attempt to make changes. Therapy can therefore be one element of a much broader ecosystem and an incredibly challenging process. More positively, it can also have a deep and meaningful impact on peoples' lives, with research suggesting that 75–80% individuals who access therapy report that they are better off as a consequence of attending it (Wampold & Imel, 2015). Whilst statistics such as these need to be treated with some caution, studies examining the outcomes of therapy do consistently reflect that many people get benefits from attending it.

As noted in the earlier chapters of this book, the profession of counselling psychology has very deep and wide-ranging roots. Further, whilst there are commonalities in the way people define it, individuals need to be open to their being a large range of ways that it might be interpreted. When thinking about the activity of offering therapy, a similar position should also be adopted. Therapy is not a new-fangled technology that has been invented by modern psychologists in the Global North. It stands on the shoulders of many traditions that have come before it. For instance, the first psychiatric ward in the world is thought to have been established in Baghdad in 705 (Awaad et al., 2019). Further, in the 1280s within Egypt, psychiatric hospitals were developed that made use of Islamic thinking to support individuals in distress. Moodley and van der Tempel (2018) outline the way in which psychologies grew in the Global South, with Afro-centric healing traditions, Chinese medicinal approaches, and Asian religious healing practices all playing significant roles in supporting others. These forerunners, and alternatives, to the therapies that are often prioritised today in Western societies are often forgotten or made use of without credit or acknowledgement by the colonial forces that now dominate.

The many theories that influence the therapy world

In the Global North, therapeutic theories in their more contemporary forms started to take shape at the turn of the 20th century. As is referred to in Chapter 1, the growing interest in supportive work, such as that Bertha Pappenheim and Joseph Breuer entered into (Breuer & Freud, 1895), might be seen as acting as another catalyst for individuals to start writing down and sharing their understandings of distress and their theories of how people might help alleviate it. There are lots of different types of therapy, each with its own distinct theory. Indeed, during the 1980s, a study exploring the number of therapeutic approaches chronicled over 500 types (Prochaska et al., 2018). These included everything from commonplace approaches that had been well defined and described in the literature

Force of psychology refers to the major historical movements that have shaped the field of psychology, each introducing distinct perspectives on human behaviour and therapy.

to those that were more speculative in nature. Whilst people seem to have stopped counting the development of new approaches of therapy, new ways to working continue to be developed. For the purposes here, we will not try to outline 500 specific approaches but, instead, summarise what are known as the core forces of therapeutic theory.

To start with, we outline the three **forces of psychology** that have been dominant in shaping the therapeutic landscape in the Global North: (i) psychoanalysis/psychodynamic approaches, (ii) behaviourism/ cognitive approaches, and (iii) humanistic-existential approaches – including the transpersonal approach. Following on from this, we then reflect briefly upon the way in which many approaches have started to be pulled together and sometimes merged and focus upon (vi) integrative approaches. To end, we go on to describe two very important dimensions of each of the previously discussed approaches. These are (iv) the transcultural dimension and (v) the social justice dimension. Whilst these latter elements might be newer contributions to the therapeutic arena, they

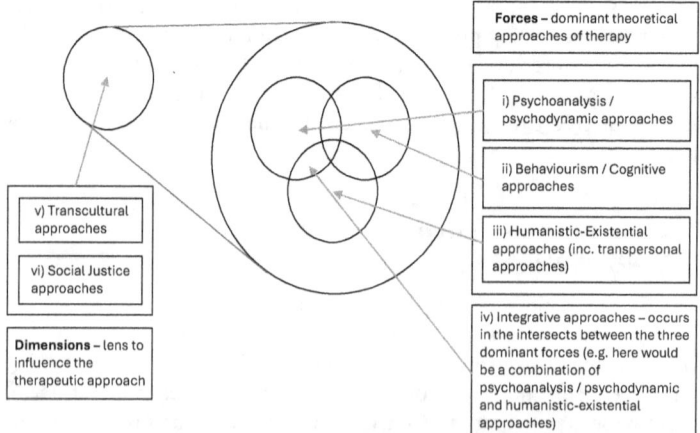

Figure 3.1 A visual representation of how the different forces and dimensions of therapeutic thinking interact.

are hugely influential to the work of counselling psychologists, with each reflecting the values of the profession that are discussed in Chapter 2. Figure 3.1 provides a visual representation of how these different approaches (forces and dimensions) might be viewed as interacting. As can be seen in this figure, the various forces might intersect to create new integrative approaches, and the dimensions reflected here can act as lenses through which individuals may make sense of the approaches themselves.

Psychoanalysis/psychodynamic approaches

Psychoanalysis is often viewed as the first force of contemporary therapeutic thinking to be developed (when viewed through a Western or colonial lens). In the late 19th and early 20th centuries, Sigmund Freud started to articulate his ideas about the nature of the human and what caused them to become distressed. He theorised that much of a human's mental life occurred outside of consciousness and that early childhood experiences and interpersonal relationships had an influence upon behaviour and mental health. Freud proposed a tripartite structure of the mind which included (i) the id – representing primal instincts and desires, (ii) the ego – which might be viewed as mediating reality and the id's more primal response, and (iii) the superego – which reflected the internalised societal norms and views of morality (Freud, 1923). Psychoanalysis was therefore devised to support people to gain a greater awareness of their internal processing, with the therapist encouraging individuals to explore their experiences (e.g. thoughts, emotions, dreams, memories) using creative approaches such as free association, dream analysis, and therapist-led interpretation. The goal of these activities was to foster self-awareness which might help empower the client to uncover and address their inner conflicts, ultimately paving the way for emotional liberation and improved mental health.

Freud's ideas formed the foundation of psychoanalysis, but his followers worked to expand, challenge, and transform his theories, often leading to very public disagreements. Key figures such as Alfred Adler, Frantz Fanon, Carl Jung, and Melanie Klein who took psychoanalytic theory in new directions. For instance, Adler's work focused on how people strive to belong and be connected to others. Fanon used psychoanalytic theory to aid our understanding of how colonialism and racism contribute to people feeling inferior and potentially accepting their own oppression. Klein pioneered object

> **Psychoanalysis** is a therapeutic approach founded by Sigmund Freud, which explores unconscious thoughts and past experiences to understand and treat emotional disorders.

relations theory which explored how early relationships with caregivers influenced emotional development. Such ideas have had huge resonance on the world of psychology and remain very present within today's psychological support landscape, with some practitioners working in ways that are aligned with the original theories, whilst others have been adapted to the context, for example,

Psychodynamic therapy is a therapeutic approach that focuses on unconscious processes, early life experiences, and interpersonal relationships.

Behavioural therapy is a therapeutic approach that focuses on modifying harmful behaviours through techniques like reinforcement, conditioning, and desensitization.

Brief Dynamic Interpersonal Therapy (Lemma et al., 2024), or have continued to develop the theories, for example, *Mentalization based Therapy* (Bateman & Fonagy, 2016). In acknowledgement of the many developments and extensions to the original psychoanalytic thinking, the phrase **psychodynamic theory or therapy** is often used as a more inclusive and overarching term.

Behaviourism/cognitive approaches

Behavioural therapy started to be developed at a similar time as psychoanalysis. John B. Watson published his seminal paper *Psychology as the Behaviorist Views It* in 1913 (Watson, 1913). In contrast to other approaches which may have prized techniques such as introspection, Watson argued that psychology should be purely objective and observable. He believed that subjective self-report findings were unscientific and unreliable. Consequently, drawing on work that investigated how to change the behaviours of animals, such as that conducted by Ivan Pavlov on his now infamous drooling dogs or Burrhus Skinner's maze-running rats, he proposed that behaviour could be shaped through a process of conditioning (i.e. certain stimuli might elicit predictable responses). This way of working became increasingly popular, and its influence grew hugely during the 1900s (Rachman, 2015). Whilst it itself has been widely critiqued, it could be seen as a less medically intrusive alternative to the procedures (e.g. lobotomies or electroconvulsive treatments) and medications being trialled within the world of psychiatry during this period.

As interest grew, the influential behavioural psychologists Hans Eysenck and Joseph Wolpe were successful in getting the journal *Behaviour Research and Therapy* accepted for publication, the first edition being published in 1963. This perspective fit very nicely with the medicalised view of healthcare that was so prevalent within hospitals at the time. It essentially adopted the idea that, like a broken leg, a faulty psyche (maybe a difficulty such as anxiety or depression) might be fixed using an appropriate behavioural intervention – for instance, a process of graded exposure to a feared object, such as a spider, might eventually reduce the symptoms of fear or distress going forward.

> **Cognitive therapy** is a type of psychotherapy that helps individuals identify and change negative thought patterns to improve emotional regulation and behaviour.
>
> **Cognitive behaviour therapy** is a goal-oriented therapy combining cognitive and behavioural techniques to address unhelpful thought patterns and behaviours that contribute to mental health issues.

Cognitive therapy, an approach that subsequently became closely aligned with behavioural psychological theories, started to gain popularity during the 1960s and 1970s, with the work of Aaron Beck (Beck, 1976) and Albert Ellis (Ellis, 1973) highlighting the way that unhelpful, distorted, or irrational thoughts might contribute to emotional distress and problematic behaviours. In their work, cognitive therapists highlight that a therapist can play an important role in understanding the automatic thoughts that people may be having and challenging any associated core beliefs. This perspective has been very successfully brought together with the action-orientated focus of behavioural therapeutic techniques. The union of these two perspectives is now being known as **cognitive-behaviour therapy (CBT)**. This is probably the most well-known approach to therapy in the Global North and has been widely researched and tailored for specific difficulties. It is now widely used in numerous countries across the globe.

CBT has many variants, with its evolution being described as going through a series of three waves to date (Mansell, 2008). This includes the first wave in which CBT might have been applied relatively separately, the second wave in which these two approaches become systematically amalgamated into what might be viewed as a stereotypical CBT approach, and the third wave which has seen the growth of cognitive behavioural approaches that have been combined with new philosophical or theoretical thinking, for instance, mindfulness-based CBT or metacognitive therapy. Each of these waves is still present within today's therapy landscape and highlights the complexity of claiming that CBT is a single, clearly defined entity. This might be viewed as even more complex when considering that Albert Ellis also described rational emotive therapy, his initial outline of an approach combining cognitive and behavioural thinking as a humanistic psychotherapy (Ellis, 1973), the next force of psychology we move on to introduce.

Humanistic-existential approaches

The third force of therapeutic thinking is often noted to be the force of **humanistic psychology** (Bugental, 1964) – a perspective that, as discussed in Chapter 2, is often viewed as a central foundation for counselling psychology. This theory was developed in opposition to the perspectives that had developed in traditional psychoanalysis and behavioural psychology. Its key proponents, people like Abraham Maslow, Carl Rogers, and Charlotte Bühler, disagreed with the existing reductionist and deterministic perspectives of the human and believed that such views neglected the full richness of human experience. In contrast, humanistic psychologists developed a statement which highlighted their belief that humans are unique, have the potential to constructively grow if they are provided with the correct environment and, in the main, are able to make choices related to their lives. The philosophical focus that humanistic psychologists take, notably considering existential topics such as why humans are unique beings in this world or what makes a good life, means that they are sometimes referred to as humanistic-existential psychologists or therapists. Further, following on from this, humanistic psychologists typically focus upon the potential a person has to change or constructively grow, a view which contrasts starkly with the previous perspectives that typically focused upon an individual's deficits. Thus, rather than being viewed as a tool to help fix a disorder, humanistic therapists focus upon creating a supportive environment for an individual to explore and learn more about themselves in the world.

There are lots of varieties of humanistic therapies. These include approaches such as Gestalt therapy, emotion-focused therapy, narrative therapy, and specific existential therapies. Probably the most well-known and applied approach is **person-centred therapy** as described by Carl

> **Humanistic psychology** is a theoretical approach which understands a person as someone who is unique, more than the sum of their parts, and who can constructively grow (i.e. to flourish and work towards reaching their potential as humans), given the right circumstances.

Rogers (Rogers, 1951) (also referred to as non-directive therapy or client-directed therapy). Within this approach, Rogers described the way that therapists would purposefully attempt to create environments that are safe spaces for an individual to explore their life.

Person-centred therapy is a humanistic therapeutic approach developed by Carl Rogers that focuses on providing a supportive, empathetic, and non-judgemental environment for clients to explore and potentially resolve their issues.

Unlike other approaches, the therapist would concentrate on *being with*, rather than *doing to* the people that they met. In doing so, the therapists would attempt to offer what have been described as the 'core conditions' of therapy (Mearns et al., 2013), notably being non-judgemental, empathic, and genuine within the therapeutic space. Whilst these three 'core conditions' are frequently emphasised in training and practice, it is important to note that Rogers originally outlined six necessary and sufficient conditions for therapeutic change (Rogers, 1957). These included not only the therapist's attitudes of congruence, unconditional positive regard, and empathic understanding but also the presence of a therapeutic relationship, the client's perception of the therapist's attitudes, and the client's own state of incongruence. As with other therapeutic traditions, the person-centred approach has evolved into a number of different strands, sometimes referred to as the various 'tribes' of the approach (Cooper, 2024). These include those that remain faithful to the non-directive stance of Rogers' original writings, and those who advocate for a more active or directive role for the therapist. Debates over these differing interpretations continue and may go some way to explaining why so many therapeutic approaches have been articulated to date.

Transpersonal psychology is sometimes referred to as the fourth force of psychology, but here we are presenting it as an extension of humanistic psychology – in part because it was a development of Abraham Maslow's thinking about humanistic psychology (Maslow, 1969). It continues along the pathway of focusing upon growth but places a greater emphasis upon the need for a bridge between the spiritual dimension of human existence and commonplace psychology in the Global North. As such, writers in this area explore topics such as transcendence (higher states of consciousness) and the relatedness or interconnectedness between individuals and the world. Transpersonal therapists, like humanistic therapists, therefore, adopt a holistic view of therapy and prize the importance of developing rich relationships with individuals. In these spaces, individuals are supported to explore their lives, and their place in the universe with a view of working towards transcendence or spiritual growth. It would therefore not be uncommon for a transpersonal therapist to integrate spiritual practices, such

> **Integrative therapy** combines techniques, theories, and principles from a variety of approaches to tailor therapy to the individual client's needs.

as mediation or prayer, into their work (Grof, 2008). Whilst never gaining the profile of the earlier forces, transpersonal psychology remains very popular with a core group of psychologists.

Integrative approaches

The idea that therapists might make use of a combination of approaches has grown considerably over more recent decades. This type of working is typically badged as **integrative therapy** and has the goal of enhancing the effectiveness of therapy. Norcross (Norcross & Alexander, 2019) describes four primary ways that therapists integrate theories: technical eclecticism, theoretical integration, common factors, and assimilative integration. Table 3.1 provides a brief summary of these approaches.

As might be evident, combining approaches that have very different philosophical foundations can be quite a complex matter. As counselling psychologists within the UK are required to learn at least two therapeutic approaches, it is however necessary for them to engage with this complexity.

Table 3.1 Summary of the major integrative approaches of therapy

Approach	Short summary
Technical eclecticism	Focuses on selecting the most effective techniques for each client, regardless of their theoretical origin Emphasises practical, evidence-based matching of methods to individual needs
Theoretical integration	Combines elements from different theoretical models to create a new, cohesive framework Aims to develop a more comprehensive and effective therapy by blending compatible ideas
Common factors	Identifies and emphasises the core elements that all effective therapies share, such as the therapeutic relationship Focuses on what works across different approaches
Assimilative integration	Maintains a primary theoretical approach whilst selectively incorporating techniques from other therapies Balances consistency with flexibility to fit clients' needs

Reflexive activity: thinking critically about therapy

The history of therapy that has been written down is dominated by white men from the Global North who were often well off. How do you think this might have influenced the shape of the dominant therapeutic forces of therapy discussed in this chapter?

A transcultural dimension

The **transcultural** dimension, or a focus that is sometimes referred to as multicultural, intercultural, or cross-cultural, has also been framed as a potential fourth force in the therapeutic landscape (Pedersen, 1990). This dimension pervades all of those that come before it and recognises the importance that the cultural and political context has an important impact on human development. In doing so, it aims to support the development of understanding and help navigate differences and commonalities in the therapy room. Importantly, this perspective acknowledges that this has often been a neglected dimension within many theories of therapy (Essandoh, 1996). Given the historical roots of many theories, they often represent a very white, male, heterosexual, and middle-class perspective of the world. Whilst this certainly forms an important part of a transcultural perspective of therapy, the omission or lack of acknowledgement of the diversity of the human cultural experience impoverishes the foundations and utility of these theories. As a consequence, the importance of both reflexive practice, in which therapists reflect upon their role within the therapeutic relationship (discussed in more detail in Chapter 2), and models of multicultural competency within therapy (e.g. Sue et al., 2022) are greatly heightened. Building from earlier work on multicultural competencies, which could be argued are too restrictive and risk being interpreted in a 'tick-box' way, approaches of cultural humility and cultural attunement highlight the importance of ongoing self-reflection, an openness and willingness to learn about the culture, beliefs, and worldview of another. These emphasise the importance of relationality and respect rather than the need to develop specific knowledge or skills.

A social justice dimension

Finally, the second dimension that we highlight here is **social justice**, a perspective that might be seen as building upon

Transcultural refers to cultural interactions and exchanges that cross boundaries and blend different cultural elements.

developments in the transcultural dimension. This dimension specifically acknowledges systemic issues such as oppression, discrimination, and marginalisation in therapeutic work (Winter & Charura,

> **Social justice** is both a goal and a process which broadly relates to things like equality, anti-oppressive practices, fairness, inclusion, and shared decision-making.

2023). It recognises the impact of factors like racism, sexism, classism, and ableism in creating psychological distress. Whilst there is a clear intersection between the transcultural and social justice dimensions, the social justice dimension explicitly aims to empower individuals and address systemic injustices where possible. It also acknowledges explicitly the political context of our social and cultural identities. In doing so, it links well-being to broader societal issues and, in addition to more traditional therapeutic activities which focus upon the individuals seeking support, might see therapists engaging in broader advocacy or politically focused work. This is something we consider further in later chapters.

Conclusion

This chapter provides a snapshot of what we believe to be a brief overview of the landscape of therapeutic theory. Therapy, at its core, might be viewed as quite a simple activity but can be understood in a multitude of ways. Here we have outlined several forces and dimensions that are commonly discussed within the context of counselling psychology. All of these are ways in which we might think about the therapeutic work we are doing. Each of these approaches has its own rich history and great depths that we would encourage you to continue reading about.

Reflexive question

1 Below are three quotes from psychologists who have written about the dominant approaches of therapy. These by no means reflect the whole theoretical approach that they have written about but provide an insight into their thinking of thinking. Read through the quote and consider which major force the author might be reflecting upon. Consider the different ways in which the authors represent their approach to therapy.

Quote 1: *In the consulting room there ought to be two rather frightened people: the patient and the [therapist]. If they are not, one wonders why they are bothering to find out what everyone knows.*

Quote 2: *When the other person is hurting, confused, troubled, anxious, alienated, terrified; or when he or she is doubtful of self-worth, uncertain as to identity, then understanding is called for. The gentle and sensitive companionship of an empathic stance ... provides illumination and healing.*

Quote 3: *The trouble with most therapy is that it helps you to feel better. But you don't get better. You have to back it up with action, action, action.*

Critical thinking questions

1   What types of difficulties do you think that therapy might be unable to offer constructive support for? Why might this be the case?
2   What reasons can you think of that would stop someone from attending therapy? Consider factors such as the individuals' personal background and the context in which they live.

Further reading and resources

- Hanley, T., & Winter, L. (Eds.) (2023). *The Sage handbook of counselling and psychotherapy* (5th Edition). Sage.
  This book provides a useful overview of lots of different therapeutic approaches. It provides a helpful introduction to the approaches and signposts to core texts for even more specific further reading.
- Masson, J. (1988). *Against therapy: Emotional tyranny and the myth of psychological healing*. Atheneum Publishers.
  A thought-provoking counterpoint to the texts that advocate therapy.
- Fernando, S., & Moodley, R. (Eds.) (2018). *Global psychologies: Mental health and the global south*. Palgrave Macmillan UK.
  A text that provides an important reflection upon the place that therapy has in a Global context.

References

Awaad, R., Mohammad, A., Elzamzamy, K., Fereydooni, S., & Gamar, M. (2019). Mental health in the Islamic golden era: The historical roots of modern psychiatry. In H. S. Moffic, J. Peteet, A. Z. Hankir, & R. Awaad (Eds.), *Islamophobia and psychiatry: Recognition, prevention, and treatment* (pp. 3–17). Springer International Publishing. https://doi.org/10.1007/978-3-030-00512-2_1

Bateman, A., & Fonagy, P. (2016). *Mentalization-based treatment for personality disorders: A practical guide*. Oxford University Press.

Beck, A. T. (1976). *Cognitive therapy and the emotional disorders*. International Universities Press.

Breuer, J., & Freud, S. (1895). *Studien über Hysterie [Studies on hysteria]*. F. Deuticke.

Bugental, J. F. T. (1964). The third force in psychology. *Journal of Humanistic Psychology, 4*(1), 19–26. https://doi.org/10.1177/002216786400400102

Cooper, M. (Ed.). (2024). *The tribes of the person-centred nation: An introduction to the world of person-centred therapies* (3rd ed.). https://www.pccs-books.co.uk/products/the-tribes-of-the-person-centred-nation-third-edition-an-introduction-to-the-world-of-person-centred-therapies

Ellis, A. (1973). *Humanistic psychotherapy: The rational emotive approach*. McGraw-Hill.

Essandoh, P. (1996). Multicultural counseling as the 'Fourth Force': A call to arms. *Counseling Psychologist, 24*, 126–137. https://doi.org/10.1177/0011000096241008

Freud, S. (1923). The ego and the id. In J. Strachey (Ed.), *The standard edition of the complete psychological works of Sigmund Freud* (Vol. 19, pp. 1–66). Hogarth Press.

Grof, S. (2008). Brief history of transpersonal psychology. *International Journal of Transpersonal Studies, 27*(1), 46–54. https://doi.org/10.24972/ijts.2008.27.1.46

Hanley, T. (2023). What are counselling and psychotherapy? In T. Hanley & L. A. Winter (Eds.), *The Sage hanbook of counselling and psychotherapy* (5th ed.). Sage.

Lemma, A., Hepworth, M., Fonagy, P., Luyten, P., & Abrahams, D. (2024). *Brief dynamic interpersonal therapy*. Oxford University Press.

Mansell, W. (2008). What is CBT really, and how can we enhance the impact of effective psychotherapies such as CBT? In R. House & D. Loewenthal (Eds.), *Against and for CBT: Towards a constructive dialogue?* (pp. 19–32). PCCS Books.

Maslow, A. H. (1969). The farther reaches of human nature. *Journal of Transpersonal Psychology, 1*(1), 1–9.

Mearns, D., Thorne, B., & McLeod, J. (2013). *Person-centred counselling in action*. Sage.

Moodley, R., & van der Tempel, J. (2018). Contexts, epistemologies and practices of global south psychologies. In S. Fernando & R. Moodley (Eds.), *Global psychologies: Mental health and the global south* (pp. 59–74). Palgrave Macmillan UK. https://doi.org/10.1057/978-1-349-95816-0_4

Norcross, J. C., & Alexander, E. F. (2019). C1A primer on psychotherapy integration. In J. C. Norcross, M. R. Goldfried, J. C. Norcross, & M. R. Goldfried (Eds.), *Handbook of psychotherapy integration* (pp. 3–27). Oxford University Press. https://doi.org/10.1093/med-psych/9780190690465.003.0001

Pedersen, P. (1990). The multicultural perspective as a fourth force in counseling. *Journal of Mental Health Counseling, 12*(1), 93–95.

Prochaska, J. O., Norcross, J. C., Prochaska, J. O., & Norcross, J. C. (2018). *Systems of psychotherapy: A transtheoretical analysis*. Oxford University Press.

Rachman, S. (2015). The evolution of behaviour therapy and cognitive behaviour therapy. *Behaviour Research and Therapy, 64*, 1–8. https://doi.org/10.1016/j.brat.2014.10.006

Rogers, C. R. (1951). *Client-Centered Therapy*. Constable.

Rogers, C. R. (1957). The necessary and sufficient conditions of therapeutic personality change. *Journal of Consulting Psychology*, *21*(2), 95–103. https://doi.org/10.1037/h0045357

Sue, D. W., Sue, D., Neville, H. A., & Smith, L. (2022). *Counseling the culturally diverse: Theory and practice*. John Wiley & Sons.

Wampold, B. E., & Imel, Z. E. (2015). *The great psychotherapy debate: The evidence for what makes psychotherapy work* (2nd ed., pp. x, 323). Routledge/Taylor & Francis Group.

Watson, J. B. (1913). Psychology as the behaviorist views it. *Psychological Review*, *20*(2), 158–177. https://doi.org/10.1037/h0074428

Winter, L. A., & Charura, D. (2023). An introduction to the handbook of social justice in psychological therapies. In L. A. Winter & D. Charura (Eds.), *The handbook of social justice in psychological therapies: Power, politics, change* (pp. 3–9). Sage.

The sources of the quotes noted above

Quote 1 came from Wilfred Bion, a psychanalyst, during a lecture in 1974 in Brazil which was published in a book summarising his Brazilian lectures published in 1990.

Quote 2 came from Carl Rogers (1980) book *A Way of Being*.

Quote 3 came from Albert Ellis and Windy Dryden's (1997) book *The Practice of Rational Emotive Behavior Therapy*.

Chapter 4

Thinking about systems

Introduction

In Chapter 3, we looked at the ways in which counselling psychologists think about therapy, and the sorts of theories which guide this. Much of this is focused on *thinking about the individual*. This chapter looks at how counselling psychologists go beyond this and *think about systems* and how this might guide our work with individuals, groups, and communities. When we say 'systems' what we mean are the factors that influence an individual beyond themselves (i.e. beyond their own understandings, thoughts, feelings, and behaviours, for example). Importantly, thinking about systems is not the opposite of thinking about therapy or counselling psychology practice. Instead, counselling psychologists extend and enhance their thinking about therapy by thinking about systems. Thinking about systems helps us think about individuals (and vice versa). Some of these systemic factors are quite 'near' influences, for example, their family, friends, school, or workplace. Some are a little less direct or further away, like extended family, communities, or the media. And some might seem even more distant, like political decisions made by people like our Members of Parliament, cultural practices, or events, or economic factors which might even extend globally (see **'ecological systems theory'**, Bronfenbrenner, 1979).

Broadly speaking, the humanistic, cognitive-behavioural, and psychodynamic approaches we introduced you to already mostly focus on the individual who we see in front of us in our counselling psychology practice, disconnected from all these systemic factors around them. That isn't to say that these theories don't consider the environment around the individual at all, but it is not

> **Ecological systems theory** is a framework which looks at how an individuals' development is influenced by the (interconnected) social structures in which they are situated at various levels of proximity.

DOI: 10.4324/9781003546733-7

commonly a core focus of that way of understanding people and distress. These traditional theories think about possible explanations for a person's distress, which are about that individual, and ideas for positive change are typically about the individual too. For example, humanistic approaches might talk about an individual's 'conditions of worth', CBT about 'unhelpful thinking styles', or psychodynamic theories about 'unconscious processes'. All these mean that we are thinking about how someone's distress is caused or continues because of something they are doing or not doing (on purpose or otherwise!). People coming to see us might then focus on learning to change their thinking, or to approach something about themselves or their life differently.

Counselling psychologists realise however that this is not always the case with distress, and in many cases, some or all the distress someone is experiencing is caused and/or kept going by other factors which are not directly about them (though it might be mediated through how they experience it). For example, our distress might be caused in part by our unstable housing situation – which is mediated by how we think about and experience this situation – but the underlying external situation in the broader social system is (at least in part) causing how we are feeling. Change might then come from other places (e.g. changing our housing), as well as, or instead of, the individual changing on their own (e.g. changing how we think about our housing). That's where thinking about systems comes in. We can think about individuals *inside* their systems – by which we mean that individuals aren't just floating around on their own in little bubbles keeping them separate from one another: they are situated within families, within neighbourhoods and communities, within cultures, and within political and economic systems. All these factors influence us and can both cause and maintain distress and can help us to grow or hinder this growth. To focus *only* on thinking about the individual (inside their bubble, cut off from anything else) means missing a significant part of the picture and separating them off from these important influences.

In this chapter, we look at *how* counselling psychologists think about systems. Just like in the previous chapter, where we saw that there are a variety of different ways of thinking (or theories) which counselling psychologists might draw upon to help them think about therapy, there are a variety of ways of thinking which we might draw upon to help us think about the system in which the individual sits within. In the next few sections, we will introduce you to a few of those. First though, we introduce you to Addi, a fictional client who we return to throughout the chapter to illustrate the way that thinking about systems might influence the work of counselling psychologists:

Addi is a 28-year-old living in Northwest England. She currently lives alone in a rented flat whilst she is trying to save up for a mortgage to buy her own home. She thinks of herself as having mixed heritage: her mum is a first-generation immigrant having come to England aged 16 from India. Her dad is white British: his whole family have lived in Leigh in the Northwest for generations, and Addi is the first to move away. She thinks of herself as Brown: everyone has always said she looks like her mum's side rather than her dad's.

She moved to Manchester at 18 to go to university and got a good 2.1 degree in English Literature with Creative Writing. Since finishing her degree 7 years ago she's struggled to hold down work, having a series of fixed-term contracts at universities. Her income just about covers her rent, but she doesn't have as much left over as she'd hoped she would, and during the winter months, things get much harder.

She's currently single, having had a few short-term relationships with men and women over the years, but nothing that has made her feel that happy. She's come to therapy after feeling really 'low' for years, after telling her GP that she struggles to sleep and doesn't find she enjoys much in life anymore.

Why are systems important? Inequality, oppression, and well-being

A starting point for systems-based thinking in counselling psychology has been seeing the ways in which inequality and injustice relate to and impact the way people think and feel. For many years, researchers have shown that inequality is bad for our well-being. **Equality** can be defined in lots of different ways, including economic equality (e.g. in terms of how much income or wealth people have), political equality (e.g. peoples' rights according to the law), equality of resources and opportunities (e.g. access to housing, healthcare and education), and relational equality (e.g. whether people are treated as equal human beings). Wilkinson and Pickett (Pickett et al., 2024; Wilkinson & Pickett, 2009, 2018) reviewed data from across the globe and demonstrated that the more unequal societies are, the worse people in those societies fare on several levels, including well-being and mental health. The bigger the inequality, the worse people's mental health on average. Importantly, this is true for everyone in those societies. It is not only those who are poorer who experience higher rates of mental health problems:

> **Equality** can be understood as relating to having equal/similar opportunities, financial, or other resources, or as being treated as a moral equal.

everyone in more unequal societies is worse off, not just the people at the bottom.

Similarly, we know that factors like racism, sexism, ableism, and other forms of discrimination and oppression all negatively impact our mental health and well-being. These 'isms' aren't just something hurtful expressed by an individual either: racism (for example) is *structural*, meaning that systems within society, such as healthcare, education, and policing, all have policies and practices which consistently disadvantage people of colour and protect the needs of white people in the UK. This means it's not just about individual people saying awful things; it's about the way our society works. Political decision-making can also impact our well-being, and this shows the way in which the broader systems we mentioned above might impact us. For example, there is research that shows the negative impact of austerity (a government policy that restricted spending on areas like welfare and communities) on mental health. We also know that wars, the displacement of people globally, and the climate and ecological crises impact the way people think and feel. Overall, as Isaac Prilleltensky (a psychologist from the United States) has said, we cannot speak about wellness without also talking about fairness (Prilleltensky, 2012).

Fairness and social justice are ideas that are *structured by politics*. So, it's important to note that the systems thinking described in this chapter is necessarily **political**. The theories of therapy introduced in the previous chapter might sometimes refer to the contribution of the environment to how someone is feeling, for example, a CBT understanding of distress will likely note if someone has been experiencing stress at work, which is impacting them. Or a humanistic understanding will recognise the family context and how this might affect someone growing up and the 'conditions of worth' they develop. The ways of thinking described in this chapter do not try to be neutral when considering these systems (e.g. our community, political, or economic context) and take as the starting position that inequality is bad for people. As the feminist phrase goes: "the personal is political". This means that, as we saw above, social, political, and economic factors are deeply intertwined with our feelings and experience of the world (Hanisch, 1970; Milton, 2018):

In an assessment with a counselling psychologist (Chris), Addi was asked about how she feels, and the situations in which she feels 'low'. Chris

Political can be understood in two interconnected ways. Politics tends to refer to systems of electoral politics, where political (small p) tends to refer to everyday structuring of power relations across society.

asked about when Addi started feeling this way, and Addi realised that it had become worse since speaking to a friend who had a new well-paid professional job and had recently bought a home. She's been struggling with thoughts of feeling like a failure and trying to figure out how she can earn more money. Together they reflected on the understanding that Addi's mood was in part connected with her feeling of being 'in-between' and unstable. Addi also spoke about the increase in racism she's experienced since she moved to a different part of the city. This led to her mentioning that her new flat also has really bad damp. Even though she's been asking the landlord to fix it, they keep ignoring her.

Reflexive activity: when policy impacts upon well-being

Well-being is not just shaped by personal choices or coping strategies, it's also influenced by policies, systems, and rules that impact people differently based on their social position.

Consider

Think of a time when a policy, rule, or institutional decision (e.g. related to education, housing, work, healthcare, immigration) impacted your well-being. This could have either positive or negative impacts.

- What was the policy or rule?
- How did it impact you emotionally, practically, or socially?
- Who would you say it benefited or disadvantaged more broadly?
- How might someone from a different background have experienced it differently?

Discussion point

How does this example help you think about the role of power, inequality, and social context in shaping mental health provision?

Social justice in counselling psychology

Within this context of inequality, oppression, and well-being, **social justice** is often said to be a core value and principle in counselling psychology, as discussed in Chapter 2. This guides us to look beyond individuals, to look at the systems and structures around them (and importantly, the relationship between the individual and this context). Social justice broadly relates to factors like equality, anti-oppressive practices, fairness, inclusion, and shared decision-making (Winter & Charura, 2023). It means, in part because of a relational understanding of equality men-

> **Social justice** is both a goal and a process that broadly relates to things like equality, anti-oppressive practices, fairness, inclusion, and shared decision-making.

tioned above, that we centre the voice and experience of the person we are working with: "Social justice is only possible when the expertise of those who are theorized about begin to have their own voices heard in all their complexity and contradictoriness" (Parker, 2014, p. 32). Taking a social justice–informed perspective in counselling psychology adds to, rather than necessarily replaces what we discussed in Chapter 3. It means thinking that social, political, and economic factors are just as important for psychologists to understand as someone's thoughts, feelings, and behaviours (Winter, 2019):

> Chris and Addi decided to write out their understanding of Addi's distress, in the form of a story, which Addi connected well with. Initially when they first started looking at the things that contributed to feeling low, Chris was focusing on Addi having changed jobs and moved to a new area, and some of the things they had identified as 'negative automatic thoughts', like when she says to herself 'I'm a failure for not being able to hold down a job when I'm almost 30' and 'I should be living in a nicer area, in a home I own'. These were things that they thought they could work on challenging in the therapy, and identifying and challenging negative automatic thoughts had been a core part of their practice training when they learned CBT. They knew that reframing these thoughts into more balanced ones which acknowledged how most people don't own a house at 28 and that changing jobs frequently had not been through choice might help Addi feel less 'down'.
>
> On reflection though, they also made sure that they acknowledged the importance of the racism (both individual and structural) that Addi had encountered in her life, and the impact that living in unstable and unsuitable accommodation has on her mental health too. Just naming these things felt important to acknowledge, even though they felt like things that could immediately be addressed by their therapeutic work.

Some authors have defined social justice in psychological therapies as an 'umbrella term' (see Winter and Charura (2023) for a range of references) that incorporates diversity, equality, marginalisation, oppression, etc. Historically, in psychology and allied disciplines (at least in the UK and other English-speaking countries), 'diversity' has often been considered when talking about mental health and distress. However, any consideration of diversity can be done in one of two ways. First (as it was traditionally done), we can position white, middle-class, English-speaking, heterosexual, and not disabled people as the 'norm' and anyone else as 'the other'. Diversity then becomes about learning how someone is 'different' from what we expect, and 'adapting' what we think we know about people and mental health to these 'others'. In Addi's case, it could be about learning how having Indian heritage influences her and considering how traditional therapeutic approaches might be adapted. The second way of considering diversity has been through an anti-oppressive or social justice lens, which understands that "[t]he rhetoric of diversity and difference depoliticize the inequalities in society" (Proctor, 2011, p. 231). Working *within diversity* with Addi would mean understanding that we each have complicated social, cultural, and political identities (we talk about this more below) and that because of our identities we have access to varying amounts of power (see Khan (2023) for more on 'working within diversity'). So instead, Addi's experience might be approached by understanding how her racialised experience, as a young woman in the UK with Brown skin, might be influenced by these power relations. This involves questioning what we really know, and, importantly, whose knowledge has been prioritised or emphasised in counselling psychology historically.

Counselling psychology has looked at itself as a discipline to consider the way that its ways of thinking and working have often excluded and oppressed whole groups of people. You may have noticed as you read Chapter 3, that many of the traditional theories which counselling psychologists make use of were developed by white men (at least, those mainly drawn upon in the UK and other 'Western' countries). Indeed, most are drawn from what are known as 'WEIRD' nations – Western, Educated, Industrialised, Rich, and Democratic. These often do not represent the voices of those who are commonly less heard, because they occupy a social position which is marginalised and oppressed, or what Roy Moodley refers to as being pushed 'outside of the sentence' (2009). Psychology as a practice has a long history of involvement in **oppression** and **discrimination**, something which has recently come to the fore, resulting in apologies from large organisations such as the American Psychological Association (APA). In recent years, in response to this, research, writing, and training have been looking to bodies of knowledge which go beyond the traditional 'WEIRD'-centric ones which have dominated psychology in the UK and beyond for years. **Decolonial theories** in counselling psychology are those which prioritise the knowledge and understanding of a culture

and try to set aside colonial theories and prac-
tices (those which are
rooted in **colonisation**
and colonialism, when
one nation subjugates
another and suppresses
local ways of thinking
and being). Decolonis-
ing psychological thera-
pies means looking at the
assumptions within our
theories and approaches
and questioning if they
really do apply globally,
or whether they only
represent the experi-
ences of those in pow-
erful positions (like the
men who founded the
approaches).

Colonisation refers to the act of set-
tlers taking over a region, and also the
exploitation and suppression of those
already there.

Decolonial theories describe ways of
thinking that aim to undo the effects of
colonisation and explore power structures that maintain colonial knowledge
and suppress other forms of knowing.

Discrimination the unjust treatment
of individuals or groups based on their
social identities or characteristics.

Oppression the unjust exercise of
power over and mistreatment of individuals or groups.

Intersectional identities and social power

We mentioned earlier in this chapter that discrimination and oppression
have a negative impact on well-being, and therefore factors like racism,
sexism, ableism, and other 'isms' are all very relevant to counselling
psychology. This leads us on to a consideration of our *social identities* and an understanding of not only our individual identity but also
how society positions us because of these identities (our *positionality*).
For example, I (Laura) benefit from several socially structured advantages: I don't need to fear holding my partner's hand when we are out
together because he is a man, and I am a woman. When I gave birth to
my children, I had far better chances of receiving good healthcare and
outcomes because I am white. Because I am currently not disabled, I
am able to access public transport without relying on (often horren-
dously unreliable) support services provided by rail companies. As a
young(ish!) mother who works full time, I have experienced sexism and
encountered barriers that make it more difficult for women and those
with caregiving responsibilities to progress. As we can see, our identity
as an individual is deeply rooted in and connected with those systems
we mentioned at the beginning of the chapter, from things like healthcare to transport, and beyond. In the example of Addi, we can see that
her experience is shaped by being a young woman and by living in poor

rented accommodation. She has a university education and strong family connections. Her experiences are also shaped by having Brown skin and a 'mixed heritage', and potentially by being bisexual. These things are relevant not because of anything inherent about those experiences and parts of her identity, but because of how society treats people who experience those things, look, or identify that way, and the power relations connected to them.

Intersectionality is a theory and analytic framework that allows us to understand how different elements of individuals' and groups' socio-political identities intersect, overlap, and combine to create particular positionalities and experiences of socially structured discrimination or advantage.

Critical race theory looks at how 'race' (which is understood socially, given there is no biological basis) influences and structures how society functions.

The term **'intersectionality'** has been popularised and is often attributed to Professor Kimberlé Crenshaw (1989). It refers to the idea that our various social identities combine and multiply, and it is not enough to look only at racism, or only at sexism, but instead to consider the coming together of these. For example, the term 'misogynoir' refers to anti-Black sexism experienced by those who are both Black and a woman (Bailey & Trudy, 2018): Black women don't only experience sexism or racism, they experience the intersection of the two. For counselling psychology, intersectionality theory is relevant because our systems thinking approach means we draw on such intersectional understandings to consider how the people we work with are positioned within their environments, and their power and privilege within society.

One of the ways in which counselling psychologists think about systems is by drawing on **critical race theory (CRT)**, which looks at how 'race' (which is understood socially, given there is no biological basis) influences and structures how society functions (Brown & Jackson, 2022; Oulanova et al., 2023). CRT looks at how whiteness is positioned as the 'norm' (as we discussed above) and therefore that those who are not racialised as white are positioned as deviating from this norm and lesser. It looks at the way in which structural racism operates in society. For counselling psychology, an important idea from CRT is 'counter-storytelling': amplifying the stories and experiences of people who have typically been ignored or silenced. Prioritising these stories means counselling psychologists need to look beyond the WEIRD traditional theories and ask what the client you are working with understands of their experience, rooted in their own social, cultural, and political positioning:

> **Liberation psychology** is an understanding of psychology that aims to connect with and re-write people's histories free from the perspective of the oppressor.

Chris and Addi explored Addi's experiences growing up with her mum and dad, and the things she learned about herself and the world from both her dad's British roots and her mum's Indian heritage. Chris learned that Addi had internalised a sense of needing to be a 'good immigrant' from her mother and her 'automatic negative thoughts' were structured through her gendered and racialised experiences.

Another useful framework to draw on when thinking about systems is **liberation psychology**, first articulated by Martín-Baró (1986), and developed by various others and in different ways, including in the form of Black liberation psychology (Jamison, 2013). Similar to CRT, liberation approaches centre on re-writing people's histories free from the perspective of the oppressor. It reminds us that the WEIRD traditional theories don't always represent the lives of those who are not white, middle-class, cisgender, heterosexual, etc. Importantly, for counselling psychology, the principle of 'denaturalisation' emphasises the critical examination of beliefs and things we take for granted, including power relations around us. This leads to 'problematisation' which means a process of listening and understanding problems faced by those who have been oppressed from their point of view, in order to highlight issues where the status quo has become regarded as natural (e.g. we might have started to see it as completely normal that some employers only issue zero-hour contracts, to the point where we don't see it as something to disrupt or suggest could be changed). The term 'conscientisation' then is the means through which liberation can be achieved: the overall process through which we understand our reality and create transformative actions to challenge inequality. Liberation approaches require that:

> [T]he psychologist becomes a witness, a partner, the one walking beside, the mirror, and the vessel of faith for the process through which those who have been silenced can discover their full potential for recall of their historical memory, undergo critical analysis, and move toward social action and change.
>
> (Torres Rivera, 2020, p. 41)

Conclusion

This chapter has introduced the ways in which counselling psychologists extend and enhance their thinking about therapy by *thinking about systems*. Social justice, intersectionality, liberation psychology, and critical race theory approaches provide ways of thinking about and understanding the complex influence of the social, cultural, and political environments on the people we work with. Importantly this thinking is reflexive and attuned to the way in which power relations are at play, and how our social positionings (those of the counselling psychologist and the people we work with) influence our work.

Reflexive questions

1 Think about your social identities and consider how these have either helped you in life or meant you've been faced with barriers. How might this impact your work as a counselling psychologist?
2 What assumptions do you have about mental health and well-being, and how people become distressed? Where do you think these came from?

Critical thinking questions

1 Do you think Chris should help Addi address her problems with damp accommodation, as part of their work together? If yes, how do you think they could go about this?
2 Should psychologists remain neutral in their therapeutic work? Can psychological practice ever be political?

Further reading and resources

* Milton, M. (2018). *The personal is political. Stories of difference and psychotherapy.* Palgrave.
    A deeply engaging text, this gives an excellent flavour of the ways in which systems influence the individuals with whome we might work with in therapy.
* Tribe, R., & Bhugra, D. (Eds.) (2025). *Social justice, social discrimination, and mental health theory, practice, and professional issues.* Routledge.
    This book provides a great introduction to the theory and practice of social justice in the context of mental health.
* Winter, L. A., & Charura, D. (Eds.) (2023). *Handbook of social justice in psychological therapies: Power, politics, change.* Sage.

This handbook gives an overview of the theory and practice of social justice–informed approaches to psychological professions.

References

Bailey, M., & Trudy. (2018). On misogynoir: Citation, erasure, and plagiarism. *Feminist Media Studies, 18*(4), 762–768. https://doi.org/10.1080/14680777.2018.1447395

Bronfenbrenner, U. (1979). *The ecology of human development: Experiments by nature and design.* Harvard University Press.

Brown, K., & Jackson, D. (2022). The history and conceptual elements of critical race theory. In M. Lynn & A. Dixon (Eds.), *Handbook of critical race theory in education* (pp. 29–42). Routledge.

Crenshaw, K. (1989). Demarginalizing the intersection of race and sex: A black feminist critique of antidiscrimination doctrine, feminist theory and antiracist politics. *University of Chicago Legal Forum, 1,* 139–167.

Hanisch, C. (1970). The personal is political. In S. Firestone & S. Koedt (Eds.), *Notes from the second year: Women's liberation* (pp. 76–78). Editors.

Jamison, D. F. (2013). Amos Wilson: Toward a liberation psychology. *The Journal of Pan African Studies, 6*(2), 9–22.

Khan, M. (2023). *Working within diversity. A reflective guide to anti-oppressive practice in counselling and therapy.* Jessica Kingsley Publications.

Martín-Baró, I. (1986). Hacia una psicología de la liberación. [Toward a psychology of liberation.]. *Boletin de Psicologia (El Salvador), 5*(22), 219–231.

Milton, M. (2018). *The personal is political: Stories of difference and psychotherapy.* Bloomsbury.

Moodley, R. (2009). Multi(ple) cultural voices speaking "outside the sentence" of counselling and psychotherapy. *Counselling Psychology Quarterly, 22*(3), 297–307. https://doi.org/10.1080/09515070903302364

Oulanova, O., Olga, J., & Moodley, R. (2023). Engaging with minoritised and racialised communities. In L. A. Winter & D. Charura (Eds.), *The handbook of social justice in psychological therapies: Power, politics, change* (pp. 10–21). Sage.

Parker, I. (2014). Madness and justice. *Journal of Theoretical and Philosophical Psychology, 34*(1), 28–40. https://doi.org/10.1037/a0032841

Pickett, K., Wilkinson, R., Gauhar, A., & Sahni-Nicholas, P. (2024). *The spirit level at 15: The enduring impact of inequality.* University of York. https://doi.org/10.15124/YAO-DE9S-7K93

Prilleltensky, I. (2012). Wellness as fairness. *American Journal of Community Psychology, 49*(1–2), 1–21. https://doi.org/10.1007/s10464-011-9448-8

Proctor, G. (2011). Diversity: The depoliticization of inequalities. *Person-Centered & Experiential Psychotherapies, 10*(4), 231–234. https://doi.org/10.1080/14779757.2011.626618

Torres Rivera, E. (2020). Concepts of liberation psychology. In *Liberation psychology: Theory, method, practice, and social justice* (pp. 41–51). American Psychological Association. https://doi.org/10.1037/0000198-003

Wilkinson, R., & Pickett, K. (2009). *The spirit level. Why equality is better for everyone.* Penguin Books.

Wilkinson, R., & Pickett, K. (2018). *The inner level. How more equal societies reduce stress, restore sanity and improve everyone's well-being*. Penguin Books.

Winter, L. A. (2019). Social justice and remembering "the personal is political" in counselling and psychotherapy: So, what can therapists do? *Counselling and Psychotherapy Research, 19*(3), capr.12215. https://doi.org/10.1002/capr.12215

Winter, L. A., & Charura, D. (2023). An introduction to the handbook of social justice in psychological therapies. In L. A. Winter & D. Charura (Eds.), *The handbook of social justice in psychological therapies: Power, politics, change* (pp. 3–9). Sage.

Chapter 5

Thinking about leadership

Introduction

It has been argued that counselling psychology's values and ethics make the discipline particularly well suited to leadership, given our emphasis on "relational, collaborative, flexible, multiculturally aware, strengths-based, developmental, contextual, and self-reflective approaches to intervention" (Fassinger & Shullman, 2017, p. 942). As early as during training, counselling psychologists find themselves in positions in which they are involved in **leadership**. Roles where counselling psychologists might have influence, disrupt, and lead include providing clinical supervision, mentoring, having oversight of specific areas of practice such as leading on managing referrals and waiting lists, chairing committees, or leading on service audit and development. Later in our careers, it might also include line management, and service leadership and development. Counselling psychologists might also lead research work as principal investigators, lead on areas of training and development for other professionals, or direct doctoral training programmes. The list of areas in which counselling psychologists might make use of their leadership skills is endless. In this chapter we consider how counselling psychologists might demonstrate leadership skills across a wide variety of settings, and the way in which the values, skills, and practices discussed already can inform this. We aim to show that leadership in counselling psychology is a space for value-led action in which we collaborate, influence and disrupt to make positive change.

> **Leadership** is the action of leading an activity, group of people, or organisation. It involves exercising influence on processes and people and disrupting systems to improve things.

DOI: 10.4324/9781003546733-8

What is leadership and where do counselling psychologists lead?

Previously, leadership was typically defined in terms of the 'great man': that some people are born to be 'leaders'. Leaders were seen to be born (not made), and some people just have what it takes in terms of skills and character (typically white middle-class men who were not disabled). This is obviously problematic for being bigoted but is also outdated in terms of leadership theory. The great man theories then progressed into thinking in terms of leadership *traits*. In these accounts, some people are born leaders, but others can learn to be leaders. Importantly, to do so, we need to acquire the right skills and characteristics (traits), which we can learn about by studying those who were born to lead. However, despite many suggestions like intelligence, creativity, assertiveness, flexibility, and trustworthiness, researchers did not find or agree on a definitive list of such characteristics that would need to be fostered in leaders. It was only from the 1940s when behaviourism had developed, having a large influence in psychology more broadly, that theories shifted to suggest that leaders are not born, they are always made. In the behaviourist accounts traits were less important, and the emphasis was placed on what people do and how they behave. Leadership became about *styles* of leading. Situational theories developed from these behaviourist accounts to draw attention to the environment around the leader (see Benmira and Agboola (2021) for a discussion on the evolution of leadership theories). In all these theories, the emphasis is placed on the leader and their role: who they are, what skills, characteristics, or traits they have, or what they do.

Whilst some elements of the behaviourist and situational theories remain, more recent leadership accounts focus on the relational, and therefore move away from the leader-only focus. Instead, attention is paid to the relationship between those doing the leading and those following, and the context and culture in which they are both situated. Theories of **inclusive leadership** consider the need for leaders to demonstrate respect, recognition, responsiveness, and responsibility (Hollander, 2009) as well as curiosity, humility, collaboration, commitment, awareness of bias, and cultural intelligence (Gupta et al., 2024). These theories also consider that leadership is co-created and therefore both leaders and followers have a shared responsibility to demonstrate these things, with leaders' modelling of this as important.

Counselling psychologists have written about inclusivity and diversity in leadership (McIntosh

> **Inclusive leadership** is a leadership style that values and prizes a range of diverse experiences and backgrounds in teams.

et al., 2019), whether or not we can relate as equals when hierarchies of leadership exist (Winter, 2019), and the concept of anti-oppressive leadership (O'Brien et al., forthcoming). Leadership is also viewed as more about a co-created *process* rather than a job title or occupational role. Whilst leadership can certainly be associated with particular job titles (Service Lead, Head of Department, Programme Director, Consultant, etc.), anyone in any role (in theory) can create change and have an influence or disrupt. To make this a little more tangible, Table 5.1 provides

Table 5.1 Examples of counselling psychology leadership roles

Leadership domain	Key responsibilities
Clinical leadership	• Leading teams within mental health services, private practices, or community organisations. • Supervising and mentoring trainee psychologists and other mental health professionals. • Developing and implementing therapeutic programmes to improve service delivery.
Research leadership	• Leading research projects that contribute to evidence-based psychological practice. • Supervising postgraduate and doctoral research in counselling psychology. • Advocating for socially just and transformative research methodologies.
Educational and training leadership	• Teaching and developing curricula for psychology training programmes. • Leading workshops and continuing professional development (CPD) for practitioners. • Shaping the future of the profession by mentoring the next generation of psychologists.
Organisational and strategic leadership	• Contributing to policy development within psychological organisations or healthcare settings. • Holding leadership roles in professional associations, such as the British Psychological Society (BPS). • Driving initiatives to improve workplace well-being and staff support.
Advocacy and public leadership	• Engaging in public discourse to raise awareness of mental health issues. • Influencing mental health policies at local, national, or international levels. • Working with charities, government bodies, or non-governmental organisations (NGOs) to improve access to psychological services.
Ethical and professional leadership	• Upholding and promoting ethical standards in counselling psychology practice. • Participating in ethics boards or review committees to ensure responsible research and practice. • Providing guidance on professional dilemmas and ethical decision-making.

an overview of the leadership roles that counselling psychologists might find themselves involved in. More meaningfully then, leadership is about this process of influence, not about occupying an occupational role or having a particular title which indicates a higher position within a hierarchy. Counselling psychology leadership practice must disrupt traditional power relations and be consistent with our values; therefore, it challenges earlier ideas of what leadership looks like.

As mentioned in the introduction, counselling psychologists need to demonstrate leadership skills as early as during training, and it is therefore not long into our journey into the profession before we find ourselves in positions which involve leadership. Trainees on clinical placements during their doctoral studies may well need to demonstrate leadership, for example, by developing and piloting new group-based interventions in services, conducting service audits and evaluations, or facilitating training for allied professionals on mental health presentations. So, contrary to what we might initially think, leadership is not just something for our managers. It is not something we only need to think about when we have been qualified for a while. Leadership involves putting to use our core counselling psychology skills, values, and practices to have a positive influence in a particular area. It also requires us to think about some additional ways of being and relating. Take the example of recently qualified counselling psychologist, Wren, who will follow through the chapter to learn more about values-based leadership in counselling psychology:

> Wren is a counselling psychologist who qualified two years ago. Since then, they have been working in an outpatient mental health primary care team. As part of routine service delivery, feedback is collated from service-users and carers and recently there have been a few issues which the service managers have been concerned about. Service users and carers have raised questions about the way the staff team engage with equality, diversity and inclusion and a few service users have written about feeling excluded and discriminated against. Wren is asked by their manager to lead on developing a new Equality, Diversity and Inclusion (EDI) team who will look at enhancing the service's performance in this area.

Reflexivity and leadership

Leadership can feel intimidating, and it can bring up things for us as human beings, for example, our previous experiences (positive and otherwise) of being 'led' and managed, and our confidence and self-belief:

> Initially, Wren feels really daunted by this new role. They aren't sure how to lead a team, and the idea of 'leadership' conjures up images of

managers they have had in the past, who mostly dictated policy and told them what they could and couldn't do. The idea of being both a counselling psychologist, with the values from humanistic psychology and social justice, and a leader felt in conflict. Wren felt really scared going into the first meeting they had planned and really wasn't sure how to hold onto the skills they had been practising and developing for years in these new situations. They didn't really feel ready to lead.

Leadership in counselling psychology needs to be **reflexive leadership**. Reflexive leadership means drawing on our reflective-practice model discussed in Chapter 2 and applying it in cases where we are leading and influencing. For us, this reflexive leadership has three core elements:

- First, we should engage in *reflection on previous experience of leadership*: including on cases where we have 'led' in the past, and those in which we have worked with others in leadership roles. Wren can think, either on their own or with a trusted colleague or supervisor, about these experiences and how they might inform how they relate to others in their new role. How might they decide how to compose the new team? How might they facilitate meetings and agree on work? What positive things have they taken away from previous leadership relationships but also what do they carry with them that might be less helpful and get in the way of making these decisions and being in this role? Particularly in cases where we carry with us strong feelings about leadership (such as the fear and feeling unprepared described above), supervision and support are paramount to support good leadership practice.
- Second, reflexive leadership should involve *reflecting on our sociopolitical identities and positionality* and how these might influence the leadership work we are doing. For example, in this case, Wren is non-binary and has experienced discrimination and oppression individually, as well as carrying with them the historical and current systemic oppression of trans and non-binary people. When leading in spaces focused on EDI, they will therefore need to navigate challenging conversations as someone who is in some regards afforded less socially structured advantages in society. Additionally, they benefit from privileges due to their whiteness and therefore it is important to remember that reflexive leadership must be intersectional.
- Finally, reflexive leadership should *acknowledge the emotional nature of leadership* and the impact it can have on others and on us. Like therapeutic work, leadership is relational and, as we describe above, involves bringing ourselves into our roles. When involved in leadership, we might have to have difficult conversations and approach challenging areas where people disagree or values and philosophies clash or

make decisions which have an impact on the lives of people we are working with. For example, a line manager might need to be involved in disciplinary situations when things have gone

> **Burnout** is a state of emotional, physical, and mental exhaustion caused by prolonged stress and overwork, often characterised by fatigue, cynicism, and reduced effectiveness.

wrong, a clinical supervisor might need to flag areas of a supervisee's work which are not going well, or directors of training programmes might need to tell students that they cannot progress in their training. Reflexive leadership requires that we reflect on how our emotions influence our leadership and how our leadership influences our emotions. The reflexive and emotional nature of leadership in counselling psychology requires us to be mindful of looking after ourselves and ensuring we minimise the risk of **burnout**.

Reflexive activity: considering the emotional nature of leadership

Given the nature of the work that counselling psychologists commonly engage in, an important element to the work of counselling psychologists is self-care. With this in mind, consider the following scenario:

> Imagine becoming a newly qualified counselling psychologist. Within this new role you have been managing a new project in which you consult with a broad range of stakeholders about ways to improve an existing service. This includes senior staff, colleagues, service users and their families. You find this activity very rewarding and believe it will lead to meaningful change in the service, but it is also exhausting due to the various challenging and sometimes difficult conversations.

Reflect upon the following question:

How might you see yourself managing the emotional demands of leading this project?

When answering this, consider:

What activities might you engage in?
What resources might you have to hand?

Counselling psychology leadership philosophy, values, and ethics

Putting aside the caveats we gave in Chapter 2 about making generalisations about counselling psychology philosophy, values, and ethics, in this section, we consider what might underpin leadership in counselling psychology, across different settings, services, and roles. Specifically, we return to humanistic psychology and pluralistic principles and consider the way in which leadership can be rooted in empathy, genuineness, a non-judgemental attitude, dialogue, and collaboration:

> One of the first things Wren does in their new role is generate further information on why and how service users and carers have felt excluded and discriminated against. They ask current and previous service users and carers to complete a brief anonymous survey to do this and have some one-to-one conversations with people who contact them directly as they wish to speak more about it. Their findings from the survey suggest that racially minoritised people coming to the service report more instances of feeling excluded, and the conversations they have indicate that this can be due to a disregard for reports of racism during initial assessments. This is important information which needs to be acted upon, and Wren decides that the first thing they need to do is to consider how to best report this back to their colleagues in the service.

The humanistic underpinnings of counselling psychology rest in part on an understanding of the individual as unique, as agentic, and having capacity for growth. Entering the new territory of leadership as a counselling psychologist might therefore involve Wren considering how they can bring these values into their work, as discussed above. It is important to remember that the humanistic understanding of people as growth-oriented is not limited to growth within therapy. Indeed, humanistic theorists wrote about the way in which we can adopt a growth-oriented, humanistic perspective, in other areas of life (e.g. education, politics, peace studies). Applying this to leadership, we suggest that counselling psychologists practising **humanistic leadership** understand that the people they work with have potential to grow, develop, and change. In Wren's EDI role, they can see the potential for growth in their colleagues and their managers, rather

Humanistic leadership is a leadership style that involves relating to others with empathy, genuineness, and a lack of judgement.

than focusing on their deficits or weaknesses. For example, Wren can report the information above back to their colleagues in a facilitative way, emphasising the findings about the team's strengths, as well as areas in which they might improve. Any reporting can be focused on specific suggestions for improvement, which are feasible and achievable.

This brings us to one notable way in which our leadership roles in counselling psychology are different from (some) humanistic therapeutic work. When we are occupying leadership roles, we have an *influence and disrupt*, and we do so consciously. Therefore, in contrast to some humanistic therapeutic approaches, the work is not non-directive (i.e. where the therapist does not lead to their own solutions or interpretations and instead follows the client) in nature, and when in leadership positions we do often have a vision or goal of where we want things to get to or end up. For example, Wren will have ideas of ways they can disrupt the current systems and make change. They might try to influence the behaviours or attitudes of their colleagues, where, for example, those behaviours or attitudes are creating or reinforcing systemic barriers, and they might work on improving processes and procedures to enhance equity. This is therefore a process in which we are not being non-directive, and we do have an agenda. This is not in principle inconsistent with counselling psychology practice more broadly, with the exception perhaps of when we are working in a very purely non-directive, client-led way. However, it does raise questions about how we manage this role and the power that comes with having an influence, which we discuss further below.

Whilst all our leadership work might not be non-directive in nature, Carl Rogers' work on person-centred counselling and his necessary and sufficient conditions for growth and development might also inform some of our thinking about leadership. For example, Wren is having difficult conversations, as we can see above, with service users and carers, about things which are very important and distressing. Reporting the information back to some service managers might also be experienced as difficult, as it might challenge their own thinking about the service they manage, particularly if they have not personally experienced racism. Within all these interactions, it is important to communicate our understanding of someone else's experience (empathy), be genuine and congruent, and try to be non-judgemental. As with all person-centred work, there will be difficulties with implementing this, and reflexive practice as described above will support the translation of these values into practice. The liberation psychology principles of critical examination (denaturalisation) and listening to those who have been oppressed (problematisation) also support this work. As is evident, counselling psychology leadership draws upon the values, philosophies, and ethics covered in Chapter 2.

When our leadership roles involve working with a broader team, such as Wren's EDI team made up of colleagues in their department, principles of collaboration and dialogue from pluralism are also important to draw on. Whether the team you are working with is newly established or has been working with each other for years, or whether you are mainly working with one individual in your leadership role (such as a supervisee), thinking about how and where we can work *together* is important. For example, when working as a clinical supervisor, we might use our first sessions with supervisees to collaboratively develop working agreements, and to establish their hopes, fears, and needs from clinical supervision. We might use skills of **meta-communication** (communicating about our communication) and talk about what it feels like when we reflect our experience of what they have said. In Wren's example, collaboration can be important to ensure that a group feels motivated and engaged in their task:

> In their first meeting, Wren spends some time with the group thinking about what everyone hopes to achieve, and the things they want to change and have an impact on. Together they draw up some 'terms of reference': how and when the group will meet, how they will decide on their focus, and what they are all expected to do between meetings. Wren decided rather than going into the first team meeting with a fixed idea on all these things, they would present their ideas (so not leaving it entirely to others) but also ensure that the team had shared ownership of the process by working together rather than imposing their suggestions.

Leaders might not always be able to engage in full shared decision-making, as we might aspire to within our therapeutic work, and sometimes we might have to take decisions that our team members do not want us to (as described above). This is once again not uncharted territory for counselling psychologists, yet we come up against reasons in clinical practice too where shared decision-making is tricky. We can learn from these experiences to inform our leadership practice. Dialogue, empathy, and congruence can all support cases where shared decision-making is less possible, and reflexive leadership will likely involve turning to sources of support such as supervision when things are difficult. Indeed, supervision for leadership practice is important, similar to our supervision for clinical practice.

Meta-communication is communicating about communication. For example, this might take the form of asking what someone was thinking when they said something, or how it felt or was experienced when you said something.

Power and anti-oppressive leadership

Proctor (2017) talks about three types of **power**, which are relevant to counselling psychology:

1 Role power: inherent in particular roles we adopt (e.g. therapist and client, teacher and student, or leader and follower)
2 Societal power: arising from the way society positions us according to our social identities (e.g. in relation to our gender, social class, ethnicity)
3 Historical power: arising from our own individual personal histories of power and powerlessness

Being in a position where we are leading something – whether it be a service audit, module of teaching, supervision, or a team or service – inevitably involves managing power dynamics and occupying a position which comes with some relative power, due to the influence we have (our role power). This is not straightforward (power relations never are), as we also have varying power relations due to our social and political identities (societal power).

Intersectionality, as discussed in Chapter 4, is important to remember here. As noted above, when discussing reflexive leadership, we also each have our own histories and experiences which inform our relations (historical power). Counselling psychology leadership should account for and consider all these types of power relations in our interactions. Consider the following two scenarios:

Wren presents her findings about the dismissal of racism in the service to the service manager (Khalid, a senior clinical psychologist), along with the senior management

Power has been defined in a variety of ways (drawing on both structural and post-structural theories – see Proctor, 2017, for an overview). Broadly speaking, it relates to the exercise of influence over others. This relates to our social and political identities, experiences of social advantage, discrimination, and oppression, and is rooted in relationships.

Intersectionality is a theory and analytic framework which allows us to understand how different elements of individuals' and groups' socio-political identities intersect, overlap, and combine to create particular experiences of socially structured discrimination or advantage.

team (a range of professionals including one other counselling psychologist, two clinical psychologists and a psychotherapist). Wren makes some suggestions regarding how the service can become more anti-racist, building on the findings from their work so far.

Wren facilitates the third EDI team meeting. A new team member, Anna (an honorary assistant psychologist) comes to see her afterwards and voices some concerns about how the meeting was run, as she felt she was dismissed and couldn't share her views and experiences.

One might provide overly simplistic analyses of the power relations in these examples of Wren's work. For example, you could suggest that Wren simply had less power in the first example, as they are two-years post-qualification presenting to a senior team of managers (focusing on the role power). However, Wren is also non-binary and is frequently misgendered in the team. There are relative power differentials often said to exist between counselling psychologists and other professionals in mental health services, such as clinical psychologists. Khalid, a racially minoritised senior man in the team, has experience of both being discriminated against due to his racialised identity and of having benefitted from socially structured advantages due to his gender and role. We can see already, just considering these very brief points that the power relations are far more complicated than relating to role power alone. Power is also relational rather than an object that one possesses.

Similarly, in the second example, we know that Anna is an honorary assistant psychologist and therefore is an unpaid member of the team, who is junior and not yet qualified as a practitioner psychologist. Wren's position of leader in the context of this group is also notable, and the simplistic understanding might be to emphasise the power they hold as the leader in this scenario. This certainly needs acknowledging, and Wren is in a position of responsibility as someone chairing the meetings, to ensure that all voices are heard, and all can contribute. However, there are likely further details relating to societal power (such as Wren's gender identity, but also perhaps other factors) and both parties' historical power, which will influence the interaction and power relations. When we engage in leadership then we should try to consider all elements of these messy and complicated power relations and try as best we can to understand and manage them. This might include acknowledging when we are benefiting from power and privilege and engaging in reflexive practices to examine any blind spots or assumptions we might have. Our communication skills, empathy, and systemic understandings are likely to support this.

Consistent with the social justice values of counselling psychology, O'Brien et al., (forthcoming) have outlined various ways in which

psychologists might eng-
age in **anti-oppressive
leadership**. In addition to
self-awareness and reflexive practice which we have
discussed already, O'Brien
et al. discuss the need
for anti-oppressive leader-

> **Anti-oppressive leadership** is a lead-
> ership style that acknowledges the sys-
> temic barriers to inclusion and aims to
> disrupt those in leadership practice.

ship to include facilitating 'critical conversations', where those in positions of
leadership create *accountable spaces* in which team members can learn, reflect,
and question current practices. In the example of Wren, it is important that
they give space in team meetings for all team members to contribute and
participate in the process of enhancing equity in their service. Team members
should be supported to reflect, learn, and challenge together. O'Brien and
colleagues also emphasise the importance of community engagement when
involved in leadership in psychology. In terms of counselling psychology
leadership, the disability activism phrase 'nothing about us without us' is useful. This is perhaps most obviously relevant when engaged in EDI work, such
as in Wren's example, but can also be applied to other leadership roles, such
as when you are a clinical supervisor or a team manager. Ensuring that we
engage *with* people and have dialogue and clear communication with those
who might be impacted by potential decisions is important in anti-oppressive
leadership.

Conclusion

This chapter has looked at the various ways in which counselling psychologists engage with leadership within their roles. Such leadership
can happen early on in our careers and is not just about managers or
those who are senior in their fields. Counselling psychology leadership
is reflexive, draws on anti-oppressive principles, and values from humanistic psychology and pluralism. Counselling psychologists influence in
various ways in their leadership roles, and therefore, this practice must be
power-informed and take account of our social and political identities, as
well as the broader culture and context of our work.

Reflexive questions

1 How do you feel when you think about yourself as a leader? What
thoughts come to mind? Why do you think you feel this way?
2 How do you think your own positionality and social identities will, or
do, influence the way in which you lead others?

Critical thinking questions

1 How do you think leaders can make decisions when their values conflict with the decision they need to make? What processes can support this decision-making?
2 How might counselling psychologists facilitate difficult conversations when in leadership roles?

Further reading and resources

- **McIntosh, M., Nicholas, H., & Husain Huq, A. (Eds.) (2019).** *Leadership and diversity in psychology: Moving beyond the limits.* **Routledge.**
  This collection explores the topic of leadership and diversity from a range of different perspectives and looks and how our intersectional identities influence our leadership in various areas relevant to counselling psychology practice.

References

Benmira, S., & Agboola, M. (2021). Evolution of leadership theory. *BMJ Leader,* 5(1), 3–5. https://doi.org/10.1136/leader-2020-000296

Fassinger, R. E., & Shullman, S. L. (2017). Leadership and counseling psychology: What should we know? Where could we go? *The Counseling Psychologist,* 45(7), 927–964. https://doi.org/10.1177/0011000017744253

Gupta, M., Kuknor, S., & Sharma, K. (2024). Is inclusive leadership a journey through tolerance, acceptance, value and celebration? – An exploratory study. *Journal of Asia Business Studies, 18.* https://doi.org/10.1108/JABS-01-2024-0057

Hollander, E. (2009). *Inclusive leadership: The essential leader-follower relationship.* Routledge.

McIntosh, M., Nicholas, H., & Husain Huq, A. (2019). *Leadership and diversity in psychology: Moving beyond the limits.* Routledge. https://www.routledge.com/Leadership-and-Diversity-in-Psychology-Moving-Beyond-the-Limits/McIntosh-Nicholas-Huq/p/book/9780367661298

O'Brien, C., Chan, K.-Y., & Winter, L. A. (forthcoming). Anti-oppressive leadership principles and practices for practitioner psychologists. In A. S. Rao (Ed.), *Rethinking leadership for clinical, counselling, and health psychologists: Managing complexity and change for thriving workplaces.* Routledge.

Proctor, G. (2017). *The dynamics of power in counselling and psychotherapy* (2nd ed.). PCCS Books.

Winter, L. A. (2019). Power and privilege in psychology: Can we have egalitarian leadership? In M. McIntosh (Ed.), *Leadership and diversity in psychology: Moving beyond the limits* (pp. 85–93). Routledge.

Part 3

Key methodologies

In this section of the book, we turn towards research. We look at the key approaches, ideas, and ways of working that underpin counselling psychology's general approach towards conducting and engaging with research.

- In Chapter 6, we look more closely at what it means to do pluralistic research and to be guided by the idea that there are multiple ways in which we might understand the topics we want to know more about. Following on from this, we consider some of the different approaches to research that might be useful to answer the different types of questions that we might be interested in.
- In Chapter 7, we examine the reflexive principles which guide counselling psychologists in their relating to and generating of different forms of knowledge. We think about the way in which our prior knowledge, assumptions, and identities might influence the way we conduct and read research, and how we can make use of this in our approach to research.
- In Chapter 8, we finish the section on research by looking at doing transformative research. This chapter considers the idea of counselling psychologists engaging with research to create change and to engage with others in our research work in a way that is consistent with our values. To end, it reflects upon how counselling psychologists make use of research to inform their psychological work on a day-to-day basis.

DOI: 10.4324/9781003546733-9

Chapter 6

Doing pluralistic research

Introduction

Psychological research has a relatively short history. Like the growth of therapy (see Chapter 3), psychology as a discipline has grown out of the work of many other arenas that have deep roots within human history. Indeed, it is commonly accepted that the first psychology lab was only created by Wilhelm Wundt in 1879, in which he set out to systematically examine the notion of consciousness. Throughout the next century within the Global North, behaviourism became a highly influential approach in psychological care, and a revolution in thinking about cognition occurred. Growing alongside this thinking, societies such as the APA (established in 1892) and BPS (established in 1901) were set up as a place for discussions about new developments in this area to occur – these two are noted as the first national societies and many more have now followed. Both the APA and BPS now define psychology as 'the study of mind and behaviour'. Importantly, the emphasis on 'study' highlights the ongoing need for research to deepen our understanding of psychological processes and the world we live in. In the landscape of human history, psychology and therapy in their contemporary form are therefore relatively new areas of exploration and, whilst our understanding of 'mind and behaviour' has increased vastly over the last century, we are still very much near the beginning of this journey.

We begin by considering how research is often approached within counselling psychology, where there is a strong emphasis on openness to multiple ways of knowing. At the heart of this perspective is the idea that no single research approach is seen as inherently superior, a stance often described as **methodological pluralism.**

Psychological research is original investigation into psychological topics undertaken to gain knowledge and understanding.

DOI: 10.4324/9781003546733-10

Whilst individual coun-
selling psychologists
may differ in their meth-
odological preferences
or areas of expertise, this
broader ethos promotes
flexibility, reflexivity,
and respect for diverse

> **Methodological pluralism** is the use
> of multiple research approaches and
> methods to capture different dimen-
> sions of a phenomenon.

research traditions. It also creates space to engage with decolonial theory, which challenges dominant Western assumptions about knowledge production and calls for the inclusion of marginalised voices, epistemologies, and culturally grounded approaches. We outline this pluralistic perspective and the rationale behind it before considering how it contrasts with the dominant research culture found in other areas of psychology, which has often prioritised specific methods or paradigms. Following this, we explore some of the major research designs commonly used by counselling psychologists. Each is introduced in turn, alongside examples of openly accessible research to illustrate the kinds of studies being discussed.

A pluralistic attitude towards research

As is outlined in Chapter 2, counselling psychologists have a pluralistic outlook to their work. Nicholas Rescher, a methodological pluralist philosopher, sums this up nicely by saying that pluralism is,

> ...the doctrine that any substantial question admits of a variety of plausible but mutually conflicting responses
>
> (Rescher, 1993, p. 79)

Just as we have already discussed, this outlook can be applied to the consideration of what therapeutic approach might be chosen by a psychologist. Similarly, such an outlook can be applied to research, with the plethora of different research designs and methodologies meaning that there can be many useful ways to explore a phenomenon of interest. With this view in mind, rather than starting from the assumption that one approach to research is automatically and always in all circumstances the best, counselling psychology researchers often start by considering what question is being asked before thinking about what methodology to adopt. Thus, if you want to explore the outcomes of a particular therapeutic intervention, a **quantitative research design** in which you can measure some sort of change might be most helpful. In contrast, if you want to explore the experiences that individuals have of a particular intervention, then a **qualitative research design** in which you might engage in rich conversations about the topic might be most helpful.

At the heart of pluralistic research lies an epistemological openness – an acknowledgement that different ways of knowing contribute to a richer and more comprehensive understanding of psychological phenomena. **Epistemology**, the study of knowledge and how we come to understand the world, plays a crucial role in shaping the methodologies researchers choose. A pluralistic stance resists the idea that there is a single, definitive way to access truth, and recognises that both positivist and interpretivist approaches can offer valuable but distinct insights. Whilst a **positivist epistemology** might typically underpin quantitative research and emphasise objectivity, measurement, and generalisability, an **interpretivist epistemology** informs qualitative research, prioritising subjective experience, meaning making, and depth of understanding. In practice, counselling psychologists might be described as often adopting a **pragmatic epistemology**, which focuses on choosing the methods that best answer the research question, rather

Qualitative research design is a methodological framework for conducting research that explores experiences, meanings, and social contexts through non-numerical data.

Quantitative research design is a structured approach to research that involves measuring variables, analysing numerical data, and identifying statistical relationships.

Epistemology is the study of knowledge and how we come to understand the world, plays a crucial role in shaping the methodologies researchers choose.

Interpretivist epistemology is a perspective that sees knowledge as subjective and socially constructed, emphasising meaning-making, context, and human experience.

Positivist epistemology is a perspective that views knowledge as objective, measurable, and discoverable through empirical observation and scientific methods.

Pragmatic epistemology is a perspective that views knowledge and truth as focused on 'what works' in any given circumstance rather than a singular or global answer.

than committing rigidly to one philosophical position. Whilst this is by no means universal, such sentiments align with the pluralistic underpinning referred to earlier in this textbook. Pragmatism views knowledge as something that is useful and action-oriented, allowing researchers to draw from both quantitative and qualitative approaches depending on the goals of the study (Morgan, 2007). This epistemological flexibility reflects the pluralistic ethos of the profession and supports a more nuanced, responsive approach to investigating complex human experiences (see Chapter 2).

Within psychological research, there can often be a tension between producing work that tells a focused, neat, and tidy story about the outcomes of research (e.g. x intervention produces beneficial outcomes with x difficulty x% of the time) and the recognition that humans are very complicated beings. Counselling psychologists, with a perspective underpinned by the values of humanistic psychology (see Chapter 2), value the notion that all humans are unique and complex. Consequently, simplifying an individual's experiences into a series of symptoms can therefore appear counter to such a position. Whilst this is certainly something to reflect upon and be mindful of, it is also important to recognise that (i) whatever the methodology adopted, the role of a researcher is to digest large amounts of information and to present it in more palatable chunks to interested others, and (ii) it would be difficult for those involved in making changes (e.g. practitioners, managers, policymakers) to do their jobs without them doing so. The compromise that many counselling psychologists come to is therefore one that attempts to be critically aware and recognise these weaknesses head-on by being transparent about the shortcomings of the work that is completed. A pluralistic researcher will thus recognise that there are many ways to answer a research question and that each approach will also be limited in numerous ways.

Given the wide range of research methodologies that counselling psychologists might make use of, good quality research might be assessed using a wide range of specific criteria (see the resources section for some useful tools for considering the quality of research). More broadly, however, a good piece of research from any design might be viewed as one that is original in focus, has been conducted with due rigour, and contributes significantly to its discipline. Such a frame is commonplace in assessments of research quality (e.g. the Research Excellence Framework (REF) makes use of this to assess the quality of research produced by academics in the UK), but it is quite value-laden. For instance, what might be viewed as original, rigorous, and significant can vary from discipline to discipline and from culture to culture. The following descriptions

Research excellence framework (REF) is a UK-based system for evaluating the quality and impact of academic research in higher education institutions.

therefore provide some sense of what these might look like from a counselling psychology perspective.

- **Originality**
  Research should contribute new insights into counselling psychology, whether through novel findings, innovative methods, or by challenging existing assumptions. It should demonstrate critical engagement with theory, reflect different voices, and explore topics that are under-researched or would benefit from exploration from a different perspective, including those relevant to cultural diversity and social justice.

- **Rigour**
  Research should be methodologically sound, using appropriate and well-justified methods. It should demonstrate ethical practice, transparent reporting, and reflexivity – including careful consideration of how the researcher may influence the research process, from agenda-setting and design through to analysis and interpretation of findings.

- **Significance**
  The research should make a meaningful contribution to policy or practice by, for example, enhancing understandings of psychological distress, therapeutic processes, or client experiences. It should aim to improve therapeutic effectiveness, inform professional practice, training or development, and reflect the values and pluralistic nature of counselling psychology in the UK.

In the next sections, we move to consider some of the types of research designs that counselling psychologists might make use of. These focus on quantitative research, qualitative research, mixed methods research, and systematic reviews.

Reflexive activity: using research to make decisions

We hope that this isn't the case but imagine that someone close to you is having a difficult time. They tell you that they are struggling to cope with everyday life following the death of a close friend. They ask you for some advice about finding appropriate psychological support. They specifically ask you what type of support is commonly helpful and are also interested in how people experience the support. Consider:

What type of research evidence would you use to inform the advice that you give?

Do you think there are any limitations to solely providing advice based on the existing research?

Quantitative research

Quantitative research can take many forms, but it typically involves measuring behaviours, experiences, or perspectives in ways that can be expressed numerically. This approach allows researchers to identify patterns, test hypotheses, and draw generalisable conclusions using statistical methods. Counselling psychologists must be familiar with quantitative research techniques and are likely to regularly make use of them, some on a day-to-day basis. Most notably psychologists may be expected to use psychometric questionnaires in the form of assessment questionnaires, measures of client experience within therapy, or measures the reported therapeutic outcome or change in sessions with clients. Counselling psychologists might use these to inform their therapeutic work with a client (e.g. it might be useful to have a conversation with a client about a questionnaire that indicates that depressive symptoms appear to be increasing) or to provide a service level evaluation when in leadership roles (e.g. to calculate a summary of the average change in symptoms of anxiety following a period of therapy).

Following on from the way in which practitioners make use of quantitative research methods in their daily work are a range of more systematic approaches. Two important design types to be aware of are the use of **practice-based evidence** and the **randomised control trial**. We will describe each briefly below.

Practice-based evidence

This refers to the evidence gathered in real-world settings (Barkham et al., 2010). As many services make use of questionnaires that are routinely collected (e.g. routine outcome measures (ROMs)) this information can provide incredibly valuable reflections upon the effectiveness of service provision. Importantly, unlike many experimental designs, they occur in a naturalistic setting. The therapy that individuals receive might therefore be more flexibly interpreted and tailored to the perceived needs of those seeking support. Whilst such work is less controlled than other designs, benefits can be that (i) the interventions are an accurate reflection of what happens in the specific workplace and (ii)

> **Practice-based evidence** is research derived from real-world clinical practice, focusing on effectiveness in everyday therapeutic settings.
> **Randomised control trial (RCT)** is an experimental study design that randomly assigns participants to treatment or control groups to assess intervention effectiveness.

they can often involve large numbers of people as they are collected in existing services, rather than being set up specifically for a study.

Randomised controlled trial (RCT)

This refers to a specific type of scientific study used to test the efficacy of therapies. Commonly, an intervention group is compared to an alternative treatment group or a control group – a group typically receiving no intervention or treatment as usual (Matthews, 2006). In many RCTs, therapy delivery is standardised to some extent, often using manualised approaches to promote consistency across participants. Sessions may be recorded and assessed by independent raters to ensure **fidelity** to the intervention model. Whilst this helps establish replicability and clarity around what is being tested, it can also introduce challenges in accounting for the flexibility and responsiveness that often characterise therapy in more naturalistic or routine clinical settings. However, it is worth noting that RCTs can also be used to evaluate more complex or relational interventions, provided the design accommodates such complexity through adapted methods and evaluation frameworks.

RCTs are sometimes described as the 'gold standard' of psychological research as they (i) minimise bias by randomly assigning people to certain interventions, (ii) attempt to control for confounding variables, and (iii) provide a helpful indication of causality. Therefore, RCTs are very highly regarded and guidelines for good practice often place the results from this type of work at the top of many **hierarchies of evidence** (e.g. the NICE develop their guidelines with this type of research playing a major role).

These two types of research are well used within the landscape of the applied psychology. Both work with a view that an indication of an individual's difficulty (e.g. the level of symptoms of depression) can be captured using a tried and tested questionnaire (e.g. the Beck Depression Inventory). This questionnaire might then be applied at different intervals, for instance:

- Several weeks before therapy when someone goes onto a waiting list

Fidelity refers to the degree to which an intervention is delivered as intended or according to its prescribed protocol or manual.

Hierarchies of evidence are ranking systems for evaluating the strength and reliability of research, often prioritising experimental designs like randomised control trials.

- At the start of therapy
- At the end of therapy
- Six months after therapy has ended

Once all the questionnaires have been completed, it is then possible to look for any trends in the scores collected. Typically, researchers might be interested in whether scores have improved during the period that a person has been in therapy – thus indicating that a person's distress might have reduced during that period. Then, if the scores do appear to be positive, have the scores remained positive for a sustained period – thus indicated that any change that has occurred may be relatively long lasting. Such results can then be compared to (i) similar scores from individuals who did not receive therapy, (ii) had a comparison intervention, or (iii) the period of time before therapy started, to see if therapy may have been the active ingredient to support this change.

With the above in mind, quantitative research can provide clear, structured, and measurable information, making it highly valuable for evaluating therapy outcomes and service effectiveness. The standardised nature of tools such as psychometric measures and RCTs allows for comparisons across different populations, helping to establish **evidence-based best practices**. Additionally, its emphasis on statistical rigour increases reliability and generalisability. However, a key weakness is that it can sometimes oversimplify complex human experiences, reducing the richness of individual stories to numerical values. More specifically, RCTs, whilst considered the gold standard, may lack ecological validity as therapy within these trials is often manualised and less flexible than real-world practice. Furthermore, practice-based evidence, whilst more reflective of real-world settings, can be limited by factors such as selection bias and a lack of strict experimental controls.

Qualitative research

Much as quantitative research can come in lots of shapes and sizes, so can qualitative research. Qualitative research often involves the collection or generation of information about people's experiences, meanings, or perspectives in a non-numerical form. This might take the form of interviews, observations, or the analysis of text or images to provide an

Evidence-based best practices are clinical and therapeutic approaches informed by the best available research, practitioner expertise, and client preferences.

in-depth reflection upon a particular phenomenon. In contrast to many quantitative designs, which attempt to create relatively simplistic storylines about things like what therapy might work best with a particular difficulty, qualitative research is concerned with understanding the complexity of human experiences within their natural contexts.

> **Descriptive qualitative research** is a qualitative approach that focuses on summarising and categorising experiences without deep interpretation.
> **Interpretative qualitative research** is a qualitative approach that seeks to understand deeper meanings, perspectives, and subjective experiences.

Popular approaches to qualitative research in counselling psychology include discourse analysis, interpretative phenomenological analysis (IPA), and reflexive thematic analysis. Each of these methods provides different ways of exploring meaning, experience, and context. For instance, discourse analysis examines how language shapes and constructs reality, whilst IPA focuses on how individuals make sense of their lived experiences. Reflexive thematic analysis, meanwhile, helps researchers establish understandings of patterns and themes across participants' narratives, allowing for a rich and nuanced understanding of psychological phenomena.

A key distinction in qualitative research is between **descriptive qualitative research** and **interpretative qualitative research** approaches. Whilst both approaches aim to uncover insights into human experience, they differ in how they conceptualise meaning, the role of the researcher, and the level of analysis applied to the data.

Descriptive approaches to qualitative research

Descriptive approaches aim to capture and present experiences as closely as possible to how participants express them. These methods work with the assumption that people can directly access and articulate their experiences in a way that researchers can faithfully document. In counselling psychology, descriptive approaches can be useful for exploring how people experience therapy, emotional distress, or personal change. These methods tend to focus on what is said rather than deeply interpreting why it is said, providing rich, first-person accounts of lived experiences.

Examples of descriptive approaches

Content Analysis – Categorises and organises qualitative data to systematically describe experiences (Drisko & Maschi, 2016)

Thematic Analysis or Reflexive Thematic Analysis (Descriptive Form) – Identifies patterns in data whilst staying close to the words and meanings expressed by participants (Braun & Clarke, 2006, 2021).

Interpretative approaches to qualitative research

Interpretative approaches acknowledge that experience is not just 'out there' to be described, but is shaped by language, culture, and social interactions. These methods emphasise meaning-making, recognising that researchers play an active role in constructing interpretations, rather than simply reporting participants' accounts. In counselling psychology, interpretative approaches are viewed as particularly useful for exploring how people make sense of their experiences, relationships, and emotional worlds. These methods often examine the ways in which people construct narratives, use language, or engage with cultural frameworks in shaping their experiences.

Examples of interpretative approaches

Interpretative Phenomenological Analysis (IPA): Balances detailed experience-near analysis with researcher interpretation, acknowledging that both participant and researcher perspectives shape the findings (Smith et al., 2021).

Discourse Analysis: Examines how language and communication shape psychological experiences, identities, and relationships (Parker, 2014).

Narrative Analysis: Explores how individuals construct personal stories to make sense of their lives and psychological processes (Josselson & Hammack, 2021).

Reflexive Thematic Analysis: In addition to the descriptive version above, RTA can also take a more interpretative stance. It proactively makes use of researcher subjectivity and critical engagement with the data to come to make sense of the data that has been collected (Braun & Clarke, 2021).

A note of caution before continuing. Rather than viewing descriptive and interpretative approaches as opposing methods, they might be best understood as a spectrum – some research remains closer to participants' direct accounts, whilst other research engages more deeply with meaning-making and interpretation. The choice of approach depends on the research question:

- If the aim is to document lived experience as faithfully as possible to how it has been described to you, a descriptive approach is likely to be most appropriate.
- If the goal is to analyse how meaning is constructed, an interpretative approach is potentially more suitable.

Both approaches contribute valuable insights into the complexity of human experience, psychological distress, and therapeutic change, helping counselling psychologists deepen their understanding of the people they work with.

Qualitative research offers unique strengths in understanding psychological and therapeutic processes. Its ability to provide rich, detailed, and nuanced perspectives allows for a deep exploration of complexity and meaning in participants' own words. Unlike approaches that focus on predefined categories or numerical data, qualitative research offers flexibility in capturing the personal and subjective nature of experiences. This makes it especially valuable for counselling psychologists, whose clients often have a wide range of experiences that don't always align with standardised diagnostic or treatment models. Qualitative research is particularly adept at exploring the lived experience of being in therapy, such as how clients interpret their progress, the therapeutic relationship, or transformative moments – elements that may be overlooked by other methods.

Whilst qualitative research is an important tool for counselling psychologists, it comes with some inherent limitations. For one, its findings are often context-specific and based on smaller samples, which may not easily translate to broader populations. The interpretative nature of qualitative analysis means that the researcher's own perspective can influence the findings, making it important to remain reflexively aware of their stance in relation to the subject matter being explored. Furthermore, whilst the primary use of qualitative research is not to establish causal relationships in the way that other approaches might, such as RCTs, it can be used to provide valuable insight into causal processes and mechanisms. It particularly excels at providing in-depth understandings of lived experience but does not typically answer questions about which interventions 'work' in a quantifiable sense. Nonetheless, qualitative research plays a critical role in the evidence base for counselling psychology. For instance, it might offer important insights into how different approaches work and indications of who they might work for. By offering deep, experience-driven insights, it complements other methodologies and ensures that research stays connected to the nuanced realities of those receiving psychological support.

Mixed methods research

In recognition of the value of both quantitative and qualitative research, some counselling psychologists engage in work that integrates both approaches, often referred to as **mixed methods research**. This approach allows researchers to draw on the strengths of each method, producing a more comprehensive understanding of psychological and therapeutic phenomena (Creswell & Clark, 2011).

Mixed methods research involves combining both qualitative and quantitative approaches in a single study to gain a more complete understanding of a topic. Greene, Caracelli, and Graham (1989) identified five key purposes for using mixed methods: (i) *triangulation* (to corroborate findings), (ii) *complementarity* (to explore overlapping but different aspects of a phenomenon), (iii) *development* (where one method informs the use of another), (iv) *initiation* (to uncover contradictions or new perspectives), and (v) *expansion* (to broaden the scope of the inquiry). For example, a *development design* might begin with a survey measuring psychological distress (quantitative), followed by interviews to explore participants' experiences in more depth (qualitative). This allows researchers to better interpret the earlier findings. An *initiation* or *exploratory design* might do the reverse, starting with qualitative interviews to understand an issue more deeply, then using those findings to develop a survey for wider use.

In a *triangulation design*, qualitative and quantitative data are collected at the same time and then brought together during analysis. A study on therapy outcomes, for instance, might combine standardised symptom scores with clients' narratives about their experience in therapy. Researchers might also use *complementarity* to highlight different aspects of experience by combining multiple qualitative approaches (e.g. thematic analysis and narrative inquiry) within a broader mixed methods framework.

Whilst mixed methods research can offer significant benefits, it is also challenging to conduct a project of this kind effectively. One key difficulty lies in integrating the two approaches in a meaningful way rather than treating them as separate components within the same study. Achieving true integration requires careful planning, ensuring that both qualitative and quantitative elements inform each other and contribute to a coherent overall understanding. In addition, mixed methods research often requires expertise in both qualitative and quantitative

Mixed methods research is a research approach that integrates qualitative and quantitative methods within a single study.

analysis, which can be demanding for researchers who are more experienced in one approach than the other.

Practical challenges also arise in terms of time and resources. Conducting both qualitative and quantitative research within a single study often requires more planning, data collection, analysis, and synthesis than using a single method alone. This can make mixed methods projects resource-intensive and complex to manage. Researchers must also consider the philosophical coherence of their approach – ensuring that their approach to knowledge aligns with their methodological choices, rather than merely combining methods for the sake of inclusivity. It can also be difficult to publish mixed methods research due to misunderstandings by **peer reviewers** about the design and the difficulty of fitting in all of the content within the word count provided by the journal (Spierings & Geurts, 2025).

Despite these challenges, mixed methods research is highly valuable in counselling psychology. By integrating different types of data, research can provide richer and more nuanced understandings of therapy processes, client experiences, and intervention effectiveness. Rather than prioritising one form of evidence over another, mixed methods research embraces the complexity of human experience, acknowledging that psychological and therapeutic phenomena often require multiple perspectives to be usefully understood. As such, it continues to be an important approach for those seeking to bridge the gap between different research methods in counselling psychology research.

Systematic reviews

A final grouping of research to consider is the **systematic reviews**. This approach provides a structured and rigorous way of synthesising existing research, making it particularly valuable in counselling psychology, where diverse methodologies and perspectives contribute to the field. Systematic reviews offer a way to bring together different types of research, supporting a

Peer reviewers are independent experts who evaluate the quality, rigour, and relevance of academic work before it is published, helping to ensure its credibility and scholarly integrity.

Systematic reviews are structured syntheses of existing research studies that follow a rigorous methodology to provide a comprehensive overview of the evidence on a topic.

pluralistic position by integrating qualitative, quantitative, and mixed methods studies. Rather than relying on a single study, systematic reviews consider the collective weight of evidence, reinforcing the idea that the whole is greater than the sum of its parts.

Systematic reviews follow a clearly defined and transparent process, typically involving a rigorous literature search, the application of explicit inclusion and exclusion criteria, and an appraisal of the quality of the studies that are ultimately included. This helps to ensure that the synthesis is rigorous, minimises researcher influence, and arguably enhances the reliability of conclusions. Unlike traditional narrative reviews, which may be influenced by subjective selection and interpretation, systematic reviews aim to be methodical and replicable, providing a trustworthy summary of available evidence.

In counselling psychology, systematic reviews serve several important functions. They can identify gaps in the literature, highlight patterns across studies, and provide insights into the effectiveness of different therapeutic approaches. By assessing a broad range of research, systematic reviews can accommodate the complexity and diversity of psychological experiences, aligning with the field's commitment to a holistic understanding of human well-being. A well-conducted systematic review not only synthesises findings but also critically evaluates the quality of existing research, ensuring that conclusions are based on robust evidence.

Quality is a key consideration in systematic reviews, as discussed earlier in relation to rigour, significance, and originality. Ensuring the quality of a systematic review involves several important steps. First, the search strategy must be wide-ranging, covering multiple databases to cast the net as wide as possible. Second, the selection process must be transparent, with clear criteria for determining which studies are included or excluded. Third, studies must be appraised for their methodological strengths and limitations, using established frameworks to assess their credibility. Finally, the synthesis process should be carefully designed, whether it involves **meta-analysis** for quantitative studies or **thematic synthesis** for qualitative research.

One challenge of systematic reviews in counselling psychology is the wide array of differences evident in the bodies of existing research of studies in terms of design. Unlike medical research, where clinical trials often

Meta-analysis is a statistical technique that combines data from multiple quantitative studies to identify overall trends and effect sizes.

Thematic synthesis is a qualitative analysis method that identifies and organises patterns or themes across multiple studies.

provide standardised data, counselling psychology research spans a wide range of methodologies and philosophical perspectives. This can make it difficult to directly compare studies or draw definitive conclusions. However, rather than viewing this as a limitation, systematic reviews in counselling psychology embrace this diversity, allowing for a more nuanced and integrative understanding of therapeutic processes.

Despite these challenges, systematic reviews remain an important tool for advancing knowledge in counselling psychology. They provide a way to synthesise existing evidence, inform practice, and guide future research directions. By upholding high standards of methodological rigour, systematic reviews contribute to the development of a strong and credible evidence base, ensuring that counselling psychology remains responsive to the evolving needs of clients and practitioners alike.

Conclusion

Pluralistic research in counselling psychology embraces the integration of multiple methodologies, recognising that different approaches provide unique and complementary insights. This includes quantitative research, which identifies patterns and measures change; qualitative research, which offers deep, experience-based understanding; and mixed methods research, which combines both to provide a comprehensive perspective. Systematic reviews further support a pluralistic approach by synthesising diverse studies, ensuring a rigorous and balanced evidence base.

Reflexive question

Below we have listed some open-access examples of research using different methodologies published by counselling psychologists. Look at the papers and consider what you like and dislike about the different types of research design. Note – we've emboldened the titles – searching for these in Google Scholar (https://scholar.google.com/) should help navigate to the full paper.

Paper 1. A quantitative randomised control trial

- Cooper, M., Stafford, M. R., Saxon, D., Beecham, J., Bonin, E.-M., Barkham, M., Bower, P., Cromarty, K., Duncan, C., Pearce, P., Rameswari, T., & Ryan, G. (2021). **Humanistic counselling plus pastoral care as usual versus pastoral care as usual for the treatment of psychological distress in adolescents in UK state schools (ETHOS): A randomised controlled trial**. *The Lancet. Child & Adolescent Health*, 5(3), 178–189. https://doi.org/10.1016/S2352-4642(20)30363-1

Paper 2. A piece of interpretative qualitative research

- Demkowicz, O., Jefferson, R., Nanda, P., Foulkes, L., Lam, J., Pryjmachuk, S., Evans, R., Dubicka, B., Neill, L., Winter, L. A., & Nnamani, G. (2025). **Adolescent girls' explanations of high rates of low mood and anxiety in their population: A co-produced qualitative study.** *BMC Women's Health*, 25(1), 49. https://doi.org/10.1186/s12905-024-03517-x

Paper 3. A piece of mixed methods research

- De Smet, M. M., Acke, E., Cornelis, S., Truijens, F., Notaerts, L., Meganck, R., & Desmet, M. (2025). **Understanding "patient deterioration" in psychotherapy from depressed patients' perspectives: A mixed methods multiple case study.** *Psychotherapy Research*, 35(3), 486–500. https://doi.org/10.1080/10503307.2024.2309286

Paper 4. A systematic review using thematic synthesis

- White, E., & Hanley, T. (2024). **Current ethical dilemmas experienced by therapists who use social media: A systematic review.** *Counselling and Psychotherapy Research*, 24(2), 396–418. https://doi.org/10.1002/capr.12678

Critical thinking questions

1 Therapy is sometimes described as an art, rather than a science. Given the topics raised in this chapter, why do you think this might be the case?

2 If you were to construct a pluralistic hierarchy of evidence to make decisions about people's psychological care, what might this look like? And how might you assess the quality of the research included?

Further reading and resources

- Hanley, T., & Winter, L. (2016). **Research and pluralistic counselling and psychotherapy.** In M. Cooper & W. Dryden (Eds.), *The handbook of pluralistic counselling and psychotherapy* (pp. 337–349). Sage.
- Smith, K., McLeod, J., Blunden, N., Cooper, M., Gabriel, L., Kupfer, C., McLeod, J., Murphie, M.-C., Oddli, H. W., Thurston, M., & Winter, L. A. (2021). **A pluralistic perspective on**

research in psychotherapy: Harnessing passion, difference and dialogue to promote justice and relevance. *Frontiers in Psychology*, 12. https://doi.org/10.3389/fpsyg.2021.742676
The book chapter and open-access paper noted above provide more reflections upon pluralistic research in counselling and psychotherapy.

* The Critical Appraisal Skills Programme website – https://casp-uk.net/casp-tools-checklists/
This website includes a series of resources to assess the quality of different research designs. It helps to consider what should be included in a strong piece of research from a variety of different perspectives.

References

Barkham, M., Hardy, G. E., & Mellor-Clark, J. (2010). *Developing and delivering practice-based evidence: A guide for the psychological therapies.* John Wiley & Sons.

Braun, V., & Clarke, V. (2006). Using thematic analysis in psychology. *Qualitative Research in Psychology*, 3, 77–101. https://doi.org/10.1191/1478088706qp063oa

Braun, V., & Clarke, V. (2021). *Thematic analysis: A practical guide.* Sage.

Creswell, J. W., & Clark, V. L. P. (2011). *Designing and conducting mixed methods research.* Sage.

Drisko, J. W., & Maschi, T. (2016). *Content analysis.* Oxford University Press.

Greene, J. C., Caracelli, V. J., & Graham, W. F. (1989). Toward a conceptual framework for mixed-method evaluation designs. *Educational Evaluation and Policy Analysis*, 11(3), 255–274. https://doi.org/10.3102/01623737011003255

Josselson, R., & Hammack, P. L. (2021). *Essentials of narrative analysis.* American Psychological Association.

Matthews, J. N. S. (2006). *Introduction to randomized controlled clinical trials.* CRC Press.

Morgan, D. L. (2007). Paradigms lost and pragmatism regained: Methodological implications of combining qualitative and quantitative methods. *Journal of Mixed Methods Research*, 1(1), 48–76. https://doi.org/10.1177/2345678906292462

Parker, I. (2014). *Discourse dynamics: Critical analysis for social and individual psychology.* Routledge.

Rescher, N. (1993). *Pluralism: Against the demand for consensus.* Clarendon Press.

Smith, J. A., Flowers, P., & Larkin, M. (2021). *Interpretive phenomenological analysis: Theory, method and research* (2nd ed.). Sage.

Spierings, N., & Geurts, N. (2025). Mixed methods, mixed feelings: A review of hurdles faced and vaulting poles to apply when wanting to do and publish mixed methods research. *Journal of Ethnic and Migration Studies*, 51(2), 1–22. https://doi.org/10.1080/1369183X.2025.2487748

Chapter 7

Doing reflexive research

Introduction

As qualitative researchers engaged in contemporary practice, we accept that the researcher is a central figure who influences, if not actively constructs, the collection, selection and interpretation of data. We recognize that research is co-constituted, a joint product of the participants, researcher and their relationship. We understand that meanings are negotiated within particular social contexts so that another researcher will unfold a different story. We no longer seek to eradicate the researcher's presence – instead subjectivity in research is transformed from a problem to an opportunity... In short, researchers no longer question the need for reflexivity: the question is how to do it.

(Finlay, 2002, p. 212)

The quote above helps us to consider the elements of what we mean by **reflexive research**: it is an acknowledgement of the researcher's presence, influence, and construction of the research process and outcomes. It is an understanding of the social context of both the research and the researcher. It is a process which unfolds, and this process is embraced rather than viewed as an unfortunate difficulty which needs to be contained or resolved. Reflexivity focuses us on the fact that we, as researchers, are "part of the world being studied"

Reflexive-practitioner model is an understanding that counselling psychology training and practice should emphasise the way in which ongoing reflection on and reflection in action contribute to our work.

Reflexive research is a process: an acknowledgement, working with, and communication of the researcher's presence, influence, and active construction of the research process and outcomes.

DOI: 10.4324/9781003546733-11

(Lumsden et al., 2019, p. 1). We acknowledge that we cannot be separated from our histories and experiences (similar to our understanding of systems in Chapter 4), and that we bring these, along with our own values into the research process and how we engage with all of the steps within this. Reflexivity in counselling psychology research is therefore consistent with the values discussed in Chapter 2 and the broader **reflexive-practitioner model** within the field.

One question arises from the first quote presented above though: is reflexive research only important within qualitative research? Counselling psychologists would argue that reflexivity is important to all research we do, whether it be qualitative, quantitative, or mixed methods. Whilst reflexive practice might have been particularly embraced and discussed within qualitative methodological literature, in part because of the (often) already existing understanding in qualitative methodologies of knowledge as being subjective and co-constructed, it is relevant to consider in relation to all approaches to research. In this chapter, we unpack further the various ways in which who we are might influence the research we do, and importantly, how we might as researchers take advantage of the opportunity offered by reflexivity and make use of it in our research practices.

Our professional knowledge and assumptions

If reflexive research is about understanding the way in which the researcher is present in and contributes to the construction of the research, it is first worth acknowledging the knowledge and assumptions that a researcher comes into the study with. Typically, when beginning a research project, you will have undertaken at least a brief review of the existing research literature. For example, if you are undertaking a master's or doctoral-level research project, you might be required to write a research proposal, which would contain within it a short literature review to locate and demonstrate the need for the research you are going to do. Alternatively, you might begin a project as someone who has been involved in numerous projects in similar years for decades. So right from the outset, before they recruit any participants or generate any data, the researcher begins the process with some existing preconceptions and knowledge based on what they have read, or previous research they have been involved in.

We might also be particularly aligned to one specific theoretical framework or a particular understanding of the topic, which will influence the way we interpret the information we come across when doing a piece of research. For example, if I am particularly grounded in CRT described in Chapter 4, I will likely bring my understanding of this, and experience thinking in this way, into my engagement with a particular piece of research. Furthermore, within counselling psychology, it is also not uncommon to be researching areas which we also work in as practitioners. We therefore might hold some preconceptions or ideas about what we might find, or the potential answer to a research question we have posed, which are rooted in those experiences as a practitioner, rather than coming from the research we are doing. Reflexivity means first becoming aware of and acknowledging these preconceptions, biases, and assumptions (which we all have as human beings!), and then considering how we might make use of them, (try to) put them to one side, and/or communicate them to the reader.

Reflexive activity: when have you been influenced?

Think of a time when your personal perspective (your background, beliefs, or experiences) shaped how you understood a situation, person, or piece of information.

For example:
You might remember being in a supermarket queue and seeing a parent speak sharply or shout at their child. Based on your own upbringing or beliefs about parenting, you may have quickly judged this as inappropriate or unkind. But later, you might have wondered whether that parent was exhausted, stressed, or managing difficult circumstances.

* Did your viewpoint help or limit your understanding?
* What might this tell you about the importance of reflexivity in research or practice?

Now reflect:

* What does this everyday example, or another one from your own life, reveal about how easily we interpret situations through our own filters? In counselling psychology, being reflexive means attempting to actively notice those filters and considering how they influence the ways we listen, respond, and make sense of others' experiences.

Take a few minutes to note your thoughts. You might want to return to them as you continue reading.

Our personal, social, and political connections to the research

As well as what we know and our academic connection to the topic, *who we are* might influence the process and outcomes of the work. We can think about that in relation to our social identities and positionalities: our gender, social class, ethnicity, and so on. We can also think about it in relation to our personal history and experiences. With both, we might consider what we share with our participants or our area of focus, and what differentiates us from them or

> **Insider researcher** is where a researcher shares one or more experiences or identities with the area of research or research participants. Increasingly, however, we acknowledge the way in which we are neither fully an insider nor an outsider to our topic of enquiry, and likely occupy the space between these two ends of a continuum.

it. The term **insider researcher** is often used to describe circumstances in which the researcher shares relevant characteristics or experiences with the participants or topic, where they might be considered a member of the same participant group. For example, several of our supervisees at the University of Manchester have researched experiences of training in counselling psychology whilst they are training themselves. They have therefore shared the experience of being a trainee in counselling psychology with their participants, and therefore in some ways can consider themselves insider researchers. Outsider researchers would then be where someone is researching the experiences of a group with which they share no experiences or identities. For example, where a white woman in her forties researches the experiences of young people of colour in relation to their experiences of therapy. In both situations, the researcher and the participants may well share *some* characteristics, identities, or experiences, but perhaps not the ones we would consider most salient to the focus or contribution of the study. In the second example, the researcher may well have been to therapy themselves and therefore share the experiences of being a client, but the fact that they are neither a young person nor a person of colour will influence the way in which they relate to the stories they hear. Similarly, if for example someone is researching the experiences of trainee counselling psychologists who have had previous experiences of sexual trauma, and they share the identity of being a current trainee counselling psychologist but have not experienced sexual trauma before, they will connect with the stories differently to someone who is a trainee counselling psychologist who has had a previous similar experience. We can already see therefore that although the insider/outsider description is perhaps useful as it allows to look at touch points and overlaps between ourselves and our participants, seeing it as a dichotomy of either/or is probably not accurate. Instead, it is perhaps more accurate to say that there is really a scale of shared experiences and identities that influence the research process to varying degrees. Dwyer and Buckle (2009) have talked about the 'space between' insider and outsider status, highlighting the complexities in forcing into either inside or outside: we are all perhaps in the space between when researching subjectivities.

There are benefits and disadvantages to both being a (relative) insider or outsider in the research process, which are important to highlight. Etherington notes that "[o]ur personal history, *when it is known to us and processed in ways that allow us to remain in contact with others whose stories remind us of our own,* can enrich our role as researcher" (2004, p. 180, emphasis added). The point that she makes is that our own personal resonance with the stories we hear can help deepen our understanding and enrich the learning. Connecting with our participants can help us to develop new ideas and perspectives, and to see points of connection in the narrative. Nevertheless, personal experience of a topic that you are researching might also be tricky for several reasons, and so it is worth exploring both the pros and cons of this and ensuring that the research can draw on your reflexive experience of the topic. If the shared experience is there, but it is unprocessed for us as researchers, there is a risk that we do not understand and gain the benefits mentioned, and we risk harming our participants, and over-identifying with the stories we hear or becoming tangled in the narratives. There are some topics that might be too raw or too challenging for us to occupy a researcher role in relation to. For example, if someone has had a traumatic birth experience which they have not yet talked through with someone, or reflected upon, and when they think about their own experience it still feels very highly charged and distressing, it might be worth considering if it is the right time to plan a research project where you are going to hear others' traumatic birth experiences. Hearing the stories might be overly distressing for the researcher, and they might not be able to see their own role in the research process. If it is overly distressing, they also might feel unable to appropriately support any participants if they become distressed.

Our social and political identities, and connected with this; our experiences of oppression, privilege, and discrimination may also be relevant. For example, it might be important to note that a researcher is motivated to do research exploring experiences of social class in counselling because of their working-class identity. This might be a shared identity, and therefore they may have some elements of an 'insider researcher' status, and it might therefore be helpful to reflect on how this influences the study. In cases where the research hopes to amplify the voices of participants who are marginalised or minoritised, and the researcher benefits from socially structured advantages, it might be particularly important to reflect upon the impact of their social and political identities. For example, if a white researcher is conducting research into experiences of racism in therapy, it is helpful to reflect on their positioning in relation to this, and the power that they hold not only through their role as a researcher, but also through the privileges afforded to them in society because of their white-ness. Examining motivations for conducting work like this is important. What are we hoping to achieve, and how do our identities influence our engagement with the issues we are talking about? For example, how does a researcher's whiteness influence their understanding and conceptualisation of racism, and why do they think they might be the right person to do this research project? Projects such as this sometimes aim to 'give voice', but we should reflect on why we think we are able to '*give*' someone a voice. Don't they already have one? Why do we think we are powerful enough to do that? We must consider how we are positioning our participants from the outset and how we position ourselves in relation to this. Reflexive research means engaging with these questions genuinely in order to move from an approach which for example keeps ideas and practices rooted in patriarchy (a system in which men holder greater power than other gender identities), or colonialism (when one nation subjugates another and suppresses local ways of thinking and being) and going to one in which researchers are more genuinely able to walk besides their participants and bear witness as in the Liberation Psychology approaches described in Chapter 4.

Making use of reflexivity

As noted above, qualitative researchers would overall now view reflexivity as something to be made use of, rather than a problem for our research. The specifics of this do vary across methodologies, however, and some approaches may more clearly want to boundary the researcher's subjectivity, whereas others might wish to embrace and develop this within the work. In either scenario, reflexive research is a practice, not just a nice idea, so we need to go beyond the words of what is described above and put something into action. This section of the chapter looks at some of the strategies or approaches used to engage with this reflexive process, to translate our reflexive research values into research action we can take.

One of the primary mechanisms through which a researcher can work with their experience, positionings, and engagement with the research is through supervision. **Research supervision** is intended to support the unfolding process of the work. Supervision meetings should pay attention to both the project management and advice on specific techniques or research approaches (i.e. the mechanics of what we do and when), as well as the researcher's personal experience of conducting the project and the reflexive process. This might involve:

- Conversations about the way in which the researcher's insider/outsider/ between status is experienced during the research. At the outset, it might involve a discussion about why the researcher is motivated to do the research and what their hopes, expectations, and aims for the project are.

- Reflecting on the emotional experience of conducting the data generation processes, like interviews or focus groups.
- Discussing how, during the analysis, a researcher feels their positionings and experiences might be informing their understanding of the data and how they are engaging with it.

Research supervision is where student researchers meet regularly throughout a project with a more experienced researcher to reflect on their work, gain advice, and direction. This is intended to support the unfolding process of the work in a similar manner to clinical supervision.

- At the end of the study, reflecting with the researcher on how they may have influenced the outcomes and how the conclusions of the work might be impacted by their experiences and who they are.

Researchers might also use research diaries or journals, where they can capture some of this in a narrative form. Creative methods can also be used, for example, I (Laura) previously worked with a postgraduate researcher who used art, including painting and drawing, in her reflexive diaries rather than words. This connected both deeply with her own experiences and the subject of the research. Therefore, it was a fruitful way for her to both process and capture her processing of the research experience. It can be useful to write (or draw or use another method) reflexively in an unstructured way, but we can also ask ourselves a series of questions as prompts to begin our thinking. For example, we might write our responses to the following questions:

1 Why do I want to conduct research in this area? What is motivating me?
2 What do I think I will find or argue?
3 Why have I chosen to answer the question using this methodological approach?
4 What do I expect people will tell me in the interviews/focus groups?
5 How does my identity influence the way I connect with the topic and participants?
6 How do my experiences inform the way I connect with the topic and participants?

Another way that people sometimes use to help bring some of their preconceptions and biases to awareness is to engage in what is sometimes called a 'bracketing interview'. This is where a researcher is interviewed on the topic of the research enquiry, sometimes using the same interview questions they plan to use with participants. Some argue that it helps a researcher to access the preconceptions, biases, and assumptions of which they are less consciously aware. The interview format, where someone is in

> **Bracketing** is a process sometimes used by some qualitative researchers, whereby they *try* to set aside their biases or assumptions to focus only on the experiences of their participants.

dialogue with another, allows for greater access to these experiences and views which might be less likely to come out when writing a research journal alone, for example (see Rolls & Relf, 2006). The **bracketing** part of the name comes from the rooting in phenomenological theory: bracketing is argued to be a process through which a researcher tries to set aside their biases or assumptions to focus only on the experiences of their participants. This is not a view shared by all researchers, however, and many would argue that it is not possible to bracket off or separate parts of ourselves in this way. Nevertheless, a bracketing interview, even without the aim of separating off the things we learn about ourselves, can be potentially another strategy through which we can consider how we are present in the research we conduct.

Not neglecting reflexivity in quantitative methodologies

As noted above and is probably clear in this chapter thus far, researchers embedded in qualitative methodologies have already written a lot about reflexivity and come up with a lot of different understandings of how reflexivity can inform and enhance our practice as researchers. In quantitative approaches, this is a relatively newer area of consideration, in part because of its positioning as objective, scientific, and controlled. Quantitative researchers have, however, reminded us of the importance of reflexivity throughout these methodological approaches also (e.g. Jamieson et al., 2023). Ensuring we are reflexive about the questions we ask in quantitative research, the designs we choose, the measures we select, and the sources of knowledge we draw upon in doing so are all important parts of reflexive quantitative approaches. Jamieson et al. (2023) remind us that it is not the case that whilst textual data is subjective, numbers are objective, and they provide readers engaged in quantitative approaches with a wide range of strategies to draw upon, from pre-registering studies to enhance transparency, to including position statements, to asking yourself a series of reflexive prompts at each stage of the research.

Communicating our reflexive research

It is also important to consider how we document or evidence our reflex-ivity in the writing up of our research: how do we communicate our reflexivity, and what is it important for readers to know? It has become common for researchers to present some information about themselves in a 'position statement' in the research, which often is presented either in the methodology or in the introduction section of a paper. This is in order that readers can interpret the researcher's understanding of the data and their analysis, in the context of their declared preconceptions, assump-tions, experiences, or identities. Elliott et al. (1999) called this "owning one's perspective" (p. 221). It might be helpful for the reader to know, for example, in a paper on researching women's experiences of engaging with mental health support whilst at a women's refuge, that the lead author and researcher is a woman who has experience managing mental health ser-vices at a variety of refuge centres. Or in the research on young people of colour's experiences described above, it could be helpful to know that the researcher was one of the very few Black women professors in the coun-try, who has their own experiences of systemic racism and discrimination. In a quantitative piece looking at the effectiveness of particular pharma-cological interventions it might be helpful to know which members of the research team have connections with pharmacological companies (these are sometimes referred to as 'conflicts of interest' researchers are required to declare). This transparency allows the reader to have a greater sensitiv-ity to and awareness of how the research may have been co-constructed, and what role the researcher may have played. Position statements need to be carefully consid-ered, however, to ensure that they are not pre-senting any information (e.g. on the researcher's privilege) without think-ing through why or how this is useful. Care should be given, par-ticularly in cases where the researcher may hold more social power than the participants, because of their identities, that position statements do not simply re-centre the researcher's power and

Position statement is a statement made by researchers in publications that explain their relevant experiences and identities, which connect them to their research, and how they think this may have influenced the project. They are often used so that readers can interpret the researcher's understand-ing of the data and their analysis, in the context of their declared precon-ceptions, assumptions, experiences, or identities.

are not treated as a 'tick box' exercise. For example, when we communicate our reflexive positioning, we should go beyond simply stating our relevant experiences and identities to also explain to the reader how these may have impacted upon and shaped our work.

Conclusion

Regardless of methodology or design, counselling psychologists aim to conduct reflexive research which considers the role of the researcher and how their knowledge and experience, and social identities and positionings, influence the research process and outcomes. Reflexive research does not claim to be objective and acknowledges the active role the researcher takes in constructing the research, generating and analysing the data and communicating the findings. The reflexive counselling psychology researcher uses research supervision, structured reflexive activities, and other support mechanisms to situate themselves for the reader and communicate their reflexive positioning and process transparently.

Reflexive questions

1   Think of a research piece of research you have done, or one you would like to do. What motivates you to do the research? How do you think your experiences, identities, and motivations might influence the research process and outcomes?
2   Counselling psychology researchers often conduct research on sensitive and emotive topics. How can you, as a researcher, care for yourself and participants when conducting research like this?

Critical thinking questions

1   What do you think are the benefits and disadvantages of being an insider-researcher (in some ways, if not all), when carrying out your research?
2   How can researchers communicate their reflexive thinking and processes, in a way that informs the reader and situates their reflexivity without becoming unnecessarily focused on their self and distracting from the broader contributions?

Further reading and resources

- Etherington, K. (2004). *Becoming a reflexive researcher: Using our selves in research.* Jessica Kingsley Publications.
  This text is an excellent introduction to engaging with reflexivity in research

- **https://www.ncrm.ac.uk/resources/online/all/?id=20808 – The National Centre for Research Methods website**
  This online resource from the National Centre for Research Methods and Dr Nicole Brown gives a useful overview and some reflective prompts to consider when thinking about reflexive research.

References

Dwyer, S. C., & Buckle, J. L. (2009). The space between: On being an insider-outsider in qualitative research. *International Journal of Qualitative Methods*, *8*(1), 54–63. https://doi.org/10.1177/160940690900800105

Elliott, R., Fischer, C. T., & Rennie, D. L. (1999). Evolving guidelines for publication of qualitative research studies in psychology and related fields. *The British Journal of Clinical Psychology*, *38*(3), 215–229. https://doi.org/10.1348/014466599162782

Etherington, K. (2004). *Becoming a reflexive researcher: Using our selves in research*. Jessica Kingsley Publications.

Finlay, L. (2002). Negotiating the swamp: The opportunity and challenge of reflexivity in research practice. *Qualitative Research*, *2*(2), 209–230. https://doi.org/10.1177/146879410200200205

Jamieson, M. K., Govaart, G. H., & Pownall, M. (2023). Reflexivity in quantitative research: A rationale and beginner's guide. *Social and Personality Psychology Compass*, *17*(4), e12735. https://doi.org/10.1111/spc3.12735

Lumsden, K., Bradford, J., & Goode, J. (2019). *Reflexivity: Theory, method and practice*. Routledge.

Rolls, L., & Relf, M. (2006). Bracketing interviews: Addressing methodological challenges in qualitative interviewing in bereavement and palliative care. *Mortality*, *11*(3), 286–305. https://doi.org/10.1080/13576270600774893

Chapter 8

Doing transformative research

Introduction

The history of psychological research has involved an abundance of trans-formation. For instance, researchers have gained fame and notoriety for their cleverly designed studies and, in some instances, patients have been permanently harmed or received sub-standard care as a direct result of researchers testing out their ideas (Miller, 2008). Such externally moti-vated or damaging work is relatively rare in today's psychology, but it remains relatively commonplace that the primary focus of research has its roots in the researcher's curiosity. Researchers adopting such a stance might view their work as research 'on' a particular group. In contrast to this, some researchers proactively work 'with' individuals or groups with the motivation to create constructive change or, to put it more bluntly, to make a difference to the lives of those people the research relates to – here we note that this might not be immediate and research findings might take some time to filter into practice. We would view this as a principle that should be at the heart of the research that counselling psychologists conduct.

Considering the notion of making a positive difference is not as straightforward as it might sound. For instance, to consider another context, it is possible to positively improve the financial wealth of a community by cutting down the trees in a rainforest, but this will also negatively impact global conservation efforts. Thus, the stance of the individual judging the impact is vitally important to understanding its ultimate value. Change, related to the work of counselling psycholo-gists, is also not value-free and it is very understandable that individuals commonly disagree on what might be viewed as the most constructive way forward. So, in acknowledging this caveat, what do we mean by transformative research?

The **transformative paradigm** of research is a framework that empha-sises the importance of social justice, equity, and the empowerment of

DOI: 10.4324/9781003546733-12

those who are seldom heard in psychological research (Mertens, 2010). Merten's also describes how researchers who use this paradigm begin with:

Transformative paradigm is a research approach focused on social justice, empowerment, and challenging power imbalances to create meaningful change.

[A]n intentional plan to challenge inequality and focus on social justice that permeates the entire research process, from problem formulation to the drawing of conclusions and use of results.

(Mertens, 2003, p. 159)

This intentional way of working means that counselling psychology researchers hold on to these concepts right from the start of the project. This includes thinking about the topic of the research, developing a research question, creating a proposal and flows throughout the project until completion, including the dissemination of the work. Such a perspective is therefore very aligned with the core values that are described in Chapter 2 and highlights the importance of being reflexive researchers (as discussed in Chapter 7) to avoid engaging in research that solely confirms a particular viewpoint. Next, we consider what this might look like in practice – what might be transformed through research and how might this happen?

Research to create change

To start, selecting a research topic within the transformative paradigm requires counselling psychologists to be mindful of the societal structures that shape mental health experiences and disparities. This can involve identifying areas where research can identify trends of inequality or amplify the voices of marginalised or underrepresented groups and lead to meaningful policy or practice changes. For instance, rather than solely focusing on symptom reduction, which can be an incredibly helpful line of enquiry, transformative research may explore systemic barriers to mental healthcare, such as economic inequality, discrimination, or cultural stigmatisation of mental health concerns. Further, researchers are strongly encouraged to engage with communities, practitioners, and service users to co-construct research priorities; such a process can help ensure that the work is relevant and beneficial to those it aims to serve. By considering such issues when devising a research project, counselling psychologists are well placed to contribute to a body of work that not only deepens understanding in a particular area but also actively fosters positive change in psychological practice and potentially the wider society.

Table 8.1 Potential research impacts across systemic layers

Systemic layer	The research might...	Example
Individual layer	... highlight things that could be shared with individuals, or those working with these individuals, to create changes in support.	Maybe in-person services during normal office hours are difficult for a particular group to access support. Web-based or out-of-office-hour services might be trialled.
Family layer	... highlight things that could be shared with families, or those working with families, to create changes in support.	Research might show that family members are unaware of how best to support individuals' mental health. Psychoeducational workshops or support groups for families could be developed.
Community layer	... highlight things that could be shared with communities, or those working in these communities, to create changes in support.	Findings may indicate that stigma around mental health prevents individuals from seeking help. Community awareness campaigns or culturally sensitive outreach programmes could be introduced.
Policy layer	... highlight things that could influence policy related to working with this group of individuals.	Research may reveal systemic barriers to accessing care, leading to policy recommendations for increased funding, flexible service models, or integration of mental health support in primary healthcare settings.

Many researchers set out with the hope that their work might be able to be used to create some sort of constructive change. The target of this change could, however, be multifaceted. As a starting point, we might return to considering Bronfenbrenner's **ecological systems theory** (Bronfenbrenner, 1979) that we referred to in Chapter 4 when considering the systems that counselling psychologists work within. Such a frame highlights how individuals, families, communities, and policy are all interrelated, with each impacting the other. It might also echo the sorts of areas that counselling psychology researchers might explicitly target with their work. Table 8.1 provides some examples of what this might look like at these different layers.

Ecological systems theory is a framework that looks at how an individual's development is influenced by the (interconnected) social structures in which they are situated at various levels of proximity.

Whilst there are other types of transformation that can occur through the completion of research (e.g. conceptual or methodological), these layers represent some of the key areas that counselling psychologists might attempt to focus on.

The importance of ethics in transformative research

For transformative research to truly create meaningful change, it must be grounded in research that is conducted with integrity and based upon strong ethical principles (see **BPS Code of Human Research Ethics** (2021) for an example of core ethical principles in psychological research with humans). This way of working includes a commitment to **informed consent**, ensuring that participants fully understand the purpose, risks, and potential benefits of the research before agreeing to take part. Transparency, honesty, and respect for autonomy are essential, particularly in research that seeks to empower individuals and communities. Additionally, safeguarding participants' **confidentiality** (unless purposefully waived) and well-being is crucial, especially in sensitive areas such as mental health and counselling psychology. Transformative research in this area can involve collaboration with marginalised or vulnerable groups, making it even more important to avoid exploitative practices and ensure that participation is voluntary and non-coercive. Given that individuals

Confidentiality is the ethical and legal responsibility to protect personal information shared during research or practice from unauthorised access, disclosure, or misuse. This may involve anonymising data, securely storing records, using pseudonyms, and limiting access to identifiable information to authorised personnel only.

Informed consent is a process in which participants are fully informed about the nature, purpose, potential risks, and benefits of a study, allowing them to voluntarily decide whether to participate.

BPS code of human research ethics is a set of guidelines developed by the British Psychological Society to promote ethical, respectful, and responsible conduct in psychological research involving human participants.

Right to withdraw is the participant's ability to leave a study at any time without any negative consequences or penalties.

might change their understanding of their involvement in the project as it evolves, the **right to withdraw** from the work is also an important element of work in this area. Additionally, ethical research also requires reflexivity (see Chapter 7), where researchers continually examine their own views on topics, power dynamics, and the potential impact of their work. Without these ethical foundations, researchers risk treating those participating in their projects as passive objects, and the research process can be experienced as disempowering, ultimately undermining the very transformation it seeks to achieve.

Aligned with the view that ethically minded decision-making should underpin any research project is the importance of independent ethical review. The research of counselling psychologists will typically go through an ethics review board. This might be associated with an academic establishment (e.g. a university) or the NHS. Such a review provides an important reflection upon whether the design of the research puts individuals (participants or researchers) at risk of harm through the research – whether this be through the research process itself or the handling of personal information by the researcher. At times, within psychological research, this might involve weighing up the potential costs and rewards for a project. For instance, an individual might become upset discussing a potential topic of interest due to a personal connection (e.g. regarding the psychological care provided following the death of a child); however, their view may be essential in understanding such an experience and considering how support might be improved going forward. The BPS (2021) also highlights the importance of **justice in research**, which includes making sure that people who are most affected by an issue have the chance to be part of research about it. This means being fair in who is included, supporting participants appropriately, and being sensitive to power differences between researchers and participants. A review board would therefore examine the planned procedures and documentation related to a project to ensure that best practices, such as those referred to above, are followed. They would also consider whether appropriate support mechanisms might have been considered and be in place if the project has the potential to upset or cause distress to individuals during the research process.

> **Justice in research** is the principle that research should be fair in its design and conduct, ensuring equitable access, inclusion, and benefit for all participants, especially those historically underrepresented or affected by the topic.

Transforming through the research process

Engaging in the research process can be a transformative experience for participants, particularly when approached in a collaborative and inclusive manner. **Co-production**, where participants are actively involved in shaping the research, can support individuals to move beyond being passive subjects to becoming key contributors (e.g. designing research projects, collecting and analysing data, and helping to share any conclusions with others). This involvement can foster a sense of ownership and empowerment, as participants see their lived experiences directly influencing the study's direction and outcomes. Additionally, when participants feel truly heard and valued, the process itself can be affirming. For individuals who have previously felt ignored or marginalised, sharing their experiences in a respectful and validating space can potentially enhance self-confidence and provide a renewed sense of agency over their own narratives.

Beyond personal validation, research participation can facilitate self-reflection and personal growth. Completing thought-provoking questionnaires or engaging in structured conversations about their experiences can help participants make sense of their past, leading to the development of a deeper understanding of the topic in question and, in some instances, even emotional growth. Moreover, research can offer a unique opportunity to connect with others who share similar experiences. Whether through focus groups, peer-led interviews, or collaborative discussions, participants may find a sense of community and mutual support, reducing feelings of isolation and fostering collective empowerment. This process can also extend beyond the research itself, as participants become more aware of their role in shaping broader social or systemic change.

Participation in research can provide those involved with new practical skills and future opportunities. Training in research methods, such as conducting interviews or developing questionnaires, analysing data, or evaluating findings, can equip individuals with valuable tools that can be applied in education, advocacy, or professional settings. This knowledge not only enhances their ability to engage with research critically but can also open doors to further study or employment. Additionally, seeing their contributions influence services, policies, or therapeutic practices reinforces the idea that their voices matter and that they can be catalysts for change. By integrating the elements discussed here (co-production, validation, skill-building, and connection), counselling

Co-production is a collaborative research approach where participants actively contribute to the design, process, and outcomes.

psychologists can ensure that research is not only about gathering data but also about empowering and enriching the lives of those involved.

Whilst co-producing research can have many benefits, it is important to acknowledge that fully co-producing research can be very challenging due to time constraints, institutional requirements, or limited resources. This might be particularly the case for researchers on professional doctorate programmes who are already juggling many different tasks. These pressures can therefore make it difficult to embed meaningful collaboration at every stage of the research process, even when the intention is there.

Reflexive activity: considering transformative research

1   **Think Back** – Recall a time when you felt truly heard. What made that experience meaningful? How might research create (or fail to create) that same sense of value for participants?
2   **Identify Barriers and Opportunities** – Consider how traditional research methods either empower or limit participants. What changes could make research more collaborative and transformative?
3   **Take Action** – List three practical steps you could take to ensure that research partners or participants feel valued and gain something meaningful from the research process (e.g. co-designing questions, offering training, or creating safe spaces for sharing).

The importance of dissemination

Arguably, a weakness with much research is that it is not translated into a form that is usable by those who have the power to make change. It is not uncommon for individuals to spend large amounts of time developing a project only for it to sit in an academic archive (a physical shelf or, more likely in recent years, a digital archive) and only get read by a limited number of other researchers. With this in mind, an important part of developing research that has the potential to transform is the need for the researcher to be proactive in **dissemination**. This is not an easy task, and it can take many forms. Indeed, the multitude of formats that it might take can lead to stagnation, with some researchers not knowing what avenues might be best to have the impact that they want. Table 8.2 provides an overview of different dissemination methods. It also noted the potential audiences for the type of work suggested.

> **Dissemination** is the process of sharing research findings with relevant audiences to maximise impact and accessibility.

Table 8.2 Different types of dissemination for counselling psychology research

Dissemination type	Description	Potential audience
Peer-reviewed journals	Publishing in academic journals ensures credibility and rigour.	Academics, practitioners, policymakers
Conference presentations	Sharing research at academic or professional conferences.	Researchers, practitioners, policymakers
Workshops and training sessions	Interactive presentations for practitioners and policymakers.	Therapists, educators, healthcare professionals
Professional magazines and newsletters	Writing for industry-specific publications.	Practitioners, policymakers, organisations
Social media and blogs	Sharing insights through platforms like Twitter, LinkedIn, or research blogs.	General public, practitioners, researchers
Podcasts and webinars	Audio or video discussions about research findings.	General public, professionals, students
Policy briefs, events, and reports	Condensed summaries for policymakers or organisations.	Policymakers, organisations, advocacy groups
Media engagement (TV, radio, news)	Presenting research through mainstream media.	General public, policymakers
Community engagement and public talks	Presenting findings in local community settings.	General public, service users, practitioners
Open access repositories	Depositing research in freely accessible databases.	Researchers, practitioners, students

Research-informed therapy

When reflecting upon the idea of transformative research, a final area to consider is the explicit bridge between therapeutic work and research. **Research-informed therapy** sees practitioners make use of research findings and potentially **routine outcome measures (ROMs)** to inform their work (Hanley et al., 2023). This can be seen as a form of transformative research because it directly influences real-world change in therapy. By embedding research into practice, therapists ensure that their interventions are evidence-based, responsive, and continuously evolving to meet clients' needs. The use of ROMs, which are used to systematically track client progress, allows both practitioners and clients to engage in a reflective process that can help to foster self-awareness and empowerment. Further, this continuous feedback loop can enhance the effectiveness of therapy by making clients active participants in shaping their own treatment journeys.

When therapists engage critically with research and integrate it into their work, they potentially contribute to a culture of transformation in mental health services themselves. Rather

> **Research-informed therapy** is a therapeutic approach that makes use of the latest high-quality research to inform clinical practice to enhance effectiveness and client outcomes.
>
> **Routine outcome measures (ROMS)** are standardised tools used to assess client progress and therapy outcomes regularly, providing feedback to support the way of working a practitioner takes and improve practice.

than seeing research as a separate academic pursuit, research-informed practice can ensure that research findings are applied where they matter most, notably when supporting those who are seeking support. This approach challenges static or one-size-fits-all treatment models by encouraging adaptability, innovation, and a client-centred focus. When combined with co-productive approaches, where clients' experiences and feedback directly inform therapeutic adjustments, research becomes a living, dynamic process that not only generates knowledge but arguably also enhances individual well-being in real time. In this way, research-informed practice goes beyond knowledge dissemination by actively shaping and transforming therapeutic experiences for both practitioners and clients alike.

Conclusion

To conclude this chapter, we would reflect upon the dynamic interplay between transformative research and counselling psychology, emphasising how this approach not only has the potential to advance theoretical knowledge but can also create meaningful, practical change. By providing an alternative to traditional paradigms of research, transformative research can help to foster a deeper self-awareness in researchers and participants, provide an applied edge to the social justice values that underpin the profession, and support more inclusive practices in psychological work. As the field of counselling psychology continues to evolve, embracing transformative methodologies can also empower both researchers and practitioners to address complex, real-world issues with greater sensitivity and impact. Ultimately, this approach strengthens the bridge between research and practice, potentially leading to more holistic and effective therapeutic interventions.

Reflexive questions

1 Reflect upon the psychological research that you have already learnt about during your studies. How involved do you think the participants of those studies were? How do you feel about that?
2 Imagine being part of a research study about a topic that you feel passionate about. You answer a series of questionnaires and take part in an interview. The researchers publish their research and use it to develop a policy briefing for the service commissioners and managers in the local area. What might this experience be like? How might it differ from a project where the research was not published or used in the same way?

Critical thinking questions

1 A colleague states that they believe that research should only be conducted by someone who is distant and objective from the subject matter. Consider the strengths and weaknesses of this position.
2 Goal-based outcome measures have become increasingly commonplace in some therapeutic services. These explicitly ask the client(s) to articulate what they hope to get from the work they enter into with a psychologist. They ask clients to grade the progress of this goal and monitor this as sessions progress. Critically consider why practitioners might make use of this type of simplistic tool.

Further reading and resources

- Mertens, D. M. (2010). Transformative mixed methods research. *Qualitative Inquiry*, *16*(6), 469–474. https://doi.org/10.1177/1077800410364612
  This paper introduces the notion of transformative research. It is an interesting methodological paper.
- Hanley, T., Winter, L. A., Gordon, R., & Scott, A. (2023). A research-informed approach to counselling psychology. In G. Davey (Ed.), *Applied psychology* (2nd ed., pp. 547–566). Wiley.
  This chapter provides an overview of how counselling psychologists might make use of research in their work.
- The Involve website – https://www.involve.org.uk/
  Involve is an organisation that advocate for public participation in activities, such as research, that might influence policy. The website includes lots of useful resources for considering this type of work.

References

BPS. (2021). *Code of human research ethics*. BPS Press.

Bronfenbrenner, U. (1979). *The ecology of human development: Experiments by nature and design*. Harvard University Press.

Hanley, T., Winter, L. A., Gordon, R., & Scott, A. (2023). A research-informed approach to counselling psychology. In G. Davey (Ed.), *Applied psychology* (2nd ed., pp. 547–566). Wiley.

Mertens, D. M. (2003). Mixed methods and the politics of human research: The transformative-emancipatory perspective. In A. Tashakkori & C. Teddlie (Eds.), *Sage handbook of mixed methods in social and behavioral research* (pp. 134–164). Sage Publications Ltd.

Mertens, D. M. (2010). Transformative mixed methods research. *Qualitative Inquiry, 16*(6), 469–474. https://doi.org/10.1177/1077800410364612

Miller. (2008). Ethical issues in psychological research with human participants. In S. F. Davis (Ed.), *Handbook of research methods in experimental psychology* (pp. 127–150). John Wiley & Sons.

Part 4

Key impacts

In this section of the book, we reflect upon the way that counselling psychology is having an impact. In doing so, we consider the various layers that counselling psychologists work across and focus on the way that the influence of their work might range from impacting upon individuals to society more broadly.

- In Chapter 9, we start very locally and consider how counselling psychologists might impact the lives of the individuals that they work with as therapists. We reflect upon the types of impact that might occur and the way that counselling psychologists might monitor them. Following on from this, we move to outline how they might impact the services in which they work. Again, some of the various ways in which this might occur are reflected upon.
- In Chapter 10, we move beyond the individual and service-level changes that counselling psychologists might be involved in. Here, we examine the influence that they might have upon communities and policy. In both realms, counselling psychologists might find themselves providing consultancy to support change in various ways. For instance, they may facilitate conversations between different stakeholders, target specific groups using social media, or contribute to calls for evidence from policymakers.

DOI: 10.4324/9781003546733-13

Chapter 9

Impacting individuals and services

Introduction

This chapter moves us away from considering the approaches to research that counselling psychologists value, to reflecting more broadly upon the impacts that they might have upon individuals and services. Whilst we separate this chapter, and the chapter that follows, from the activities that counselling psychologists engage in, we view the impacts as the consequences of the various activities that are discussed in other chapters (e.g. therapy, systemic work, leadership, and research).

Supporting individuals to make constructive change

The impact that counselling psychologists can have upon the lives of individuals can be quite wide and varied. In many ways, this is often the impact that is in the foreground of the work that psychologists engage in, and if someone created a story about the work a therapist, they might characterise them as the hero of the tale. If this were the case, do you think that would represent what happened correctly? Well, it might come as no surprise that in answering this question, we would say the situation is a lot more complex than that. It is true that counselling psychologists who offer therapy to others are skilled helpers and **experts by profession**. They have been trained to offer psychological support in line with a number of therapeutic theories which have evidence bases to suggest that they are beneficial for some individuals who seek out support (see Chapter 3 for an overview of this). But, for constructive change to

> **Experts by profession** are professionals with specialised training and qualifications who apply their expertise in a given field, such as counselling psychology.

DOI: 10.4324/9781003546733-14

truly occur in somebody's life, this cannot happen without the investment and efforts of the client themselves. Ultimately, whilst the therapeutic environment and time might have been essential for the individual accessing support, it is most likely to be their actions or changes that determine whether therapy has been helpful or not. This is not to say that a therapist can do no wrong and that there is no bad therapy. There certainly is, and this can certainly inhibit constructive change or indeed cause harm to individuals (Parry et al., 2016). We would argue, however, that where positive change does occur, it is not the counselling psychologist themselves who make the changes. As a consequence, if we return to the tale about therapy noted above, maybe it is best to characterise the client as the hero in the story, a description that is used by the American psychologists Duncan, Miller, and Sparks in their book entitled 'The Heroic Client' (Duncan et al., 2004).

Although a counselling psychologist doesn't profess to make the changes in a person's life, working with one might support an individual to make significant constructive changes. Below we outline some of the ways that individuals may be impacted by engaging in work with a counselling psychologist.

Reducing negative symptoms and alleviating distress

One of the most immediate and tangible impacts of counselling psychology is the reduction of negative symptoms associated with psychological distress. Many individuals seek therapy to manage issues such as anxiety, depression, trauma, or distressing thought patterns that interfere with their daily lives. Counselling psychologists work in a research-informed way to support clients to better understand and regulate emotions, challenge unhelpful cognitive distortions, and develop healthier behavioural patterns. By being flexible and working collaboratively to address these difficulties, individuals can experience a decrease in symptoms such as persistent low mood, excessive worry, and intrusive thoughts. Whilst therapy does not typically get rid of a person's distress entirely, it can equip individuals with tools to manage their symptoms more effectively, a process which can enhance their overall quality of life and ability to function in everyday situations.

For example, a counselling psychologist working with a client experiencing chronic anxiety might use cognitive-behavioural techniques to help them identify and challenge catastrophic thinking patterns. Over time, the client may begin to recognise when they are engaging in unhelpful rumination and use grounding strategies to refocus on the present. The psychologist might observe changes through the client's self-reports, a reduction in distress scores on routine outcome measures, or improvements in daily functioning, such as the client feeling more confident in social situations or sleeping better. These indicators suggest that therapy is having a meaningful impact, even if moments of anxiety still arise.

Facilitating self-understanding and personal growth

A key impact of counselling psychology is helping individuals to gain deeper self-awareness and understanding of their emotions, thoughts, and behaviours. By providing a therapeutic relationship that is safe and caring towards the client, counselling psychologists can support individuals to explore their experiences, identify patterns in their lives, and make sense of past and present challenges that they encounter. This reflective work can lead to increased self-acceptance and confidence, allowing individuals to develop healthier coping strategies and make more intentional life choices. As noted earlier, rather than providing direct solutions, counselling psychologists make use of a variety of therapeutic theories to facilitate a space where clients can explore possibilities, challenge limiting beliefs, and recognise their own capacity for change. This empowerment can be fundamental to lasting self-understanding personal growth.

For example, a counselling psychologist working with a client who struggles with low self-esteem may use **person-centred therapy** to help them explore the origins of their self-critical thoughts. Through this type of reflective conversation and gentle questioning, the client might begin to recognise how past experiences have shaped their self-perception and start to challenge the belief that they are not 'good enough'. Over time, the psychologist may notice changes in how the client speaks about themselves, increased confidence in making decisions, or a greater willingness to pursue personal goals. These shifts, whether expressed through verbal insights, behavioural changes, or a heightened recognition of their emotional processes, can indicate meaningful self-understanding and personal growth.

Support whilst adjusting to life transitions

Counselling psychologists play a crucial role in supporting individuals as they navigate significant life transitions, such as bereavement, illness, or career changes. These experiences can be emotionally challenging, often bringing feelings of grief, uncertainty, or a loss of identity. Through therapy, individuals are given a space to process their emotions, explore the impact of change, and develop coping

> **Person-centred therapy** is a humanistic approach that emphasises empathy, acceptance, and a non-directive stance to support personal growth.

strategies that support adjustment. Counselling psychologists might use a range of approaches, such as **acceptance and commitment therapy (ACT)**, or **narrative therapy**, to help individuals make sense of their experiences and find a way forward. Whilst they do not eliminate the challenges of life transitions, they provide psy-

Acceptance and commitment therapy (ACT) is a therapeutic approach that helps individuals accept difficult emotions whilst committing to value-driven actions.

Narrative therapy is a therapeutic approach that helps individuals reshape their identities by exploring and reauthoring the stories they tell about their lives.

chological tools and emotional support that can enable individuals to adapt, rebuild their support structures, and regain a sense of purpose.

For instance, a counselling psychologist working with someone who has recently lost a partner may help them to process their grief whilst also adjusting to life without them. Through therapy, the client might explore their emotions, reflect on their changing identity, and identify ways to maintain a sense of connection with their loved one whilst moving forward with their own lives. Over time, the psychologist may notice changes in the client's ability to engage in daily activities, reconnect with social support networks, or express hope for the future. These shifts indicate that, whilst grief remains, the client is beginning to adjust and rebuild a meaningful life beyond their loss.

Supporting those who have survived significant trauma

Counselling psychologists can play a crucial role in helping individuals process and recover from traumatic experiences. Trauma can deeply impact a person's sense of safety, identity, and ability to trust others, often leading to distressing symptoms such as flashbacks, hypervigilance, dissociation, or emotional numbness. Using trauma-informed approaches, counselling psychologists provide a safe and validating space where individuals have the opportunity to process their experiences at their own pace. They help clients regulate overwhelming emotions, reframe unhelpful beliefs, and develop coping strategies that can promote resilience. Over time, therapy can support trauma survivors in reclaiming a sense of control over their lives, reducing distress, and potentially fostering post-traumatic growth. Whilst therapy does not erase the trauma, it can help individuals integrate their experiences in a way that allows them to move forward with greater strength and self-compassion.

A counselling psychologist working with a firefighter who has experienced repeated exposure to traumatic incidents might use a trauma-informed approach, such as **eye movement desensitisation and reprocessing (EMDR)** or **trauma-focused cognitive behavioural therapy (TF-CBT)**, to help them process distressing memories. The firefighter may initially struggle with flashbacks, heightened anxiety, and emotional numbing,

> **Eye movement desensitisation and reprocessing (EMDR)** is a structured therapy that helps individuals process traumatic memories using bilateral stimulation, such as guided eye movements.
>
> **Trauma-focused cognitive behavioural therapy (TF-CBT)** is an evidence-based therapy that helps individuals process and manage trauma-related distress through cognitive and behavioural techniques.

making it difficult to engage in work and personal relationships. By attending therapy sessions, they may begin to recognise triggers, develop grounding techniques, and reframe unhelpful beliefs about their experiences. Progress might be observed through a reduction in intrusive thoughts, an improved ability to manage emotional responses on the job, and a renewed sense of purpose in their role. These changes indicate that the individual is not only coping better with past trauma but also building resilience for future challenges in their demanding profession.

Encouraging agency and empowerment

Arguably, one of the most meaningful contributions of counselling psychology is encouraging individuals to reclaim a sense of agency in their lives. Many clients seek therapy during periods of distress, uncertainty, or feeling stuck in unhelpful patterns. Through collaboration, counselling psychologists help individuals identify their strengths, set meaningful goals, and develop strategies to overcome obstacles. Rather than positioning themselves as the expert who dictates solutions, they support and guide clients in discovering their own insights and resources. This approach can reinforce the idea that change is possible and that individuals have the power to shape their own lives, potentially making therapy a truly transformative experience.

For example, a counselling psychologist working with a client who feels trapped in an unfulfilling job might use **solution-focused therapy** techniques to help them identify their strengths and explore new possibilities. Through guided reflection and goal-setting exercises, the client may begin to recognise their own ability to make changes, whether by setting boundaries at work, seeking additional training, or exploring alternative career paths. The psychologist might see or hear about goals being achieved when completing **goal-based outcome measures**, see shifts in the

Goal-based outcome measures are tools used in therapy to assess progress by tracking changes in client-defined goals over time.

Solution-focused therapy is a brief, goal-oriented approach that helps clients identify and build on their strengths to create positive change.

client's language, such as moving from 'I have no control' to 'I can take small steps towards change', or see increased motivation in their actions. These signs suggest that the client is reclaiming agency and developing the confidence to take meaningful steps towards a more fulfilling life.

Advocacy and referring to other services

Counselling psychologists can play an important role in advocating for clients, ensuring they receive the support and resources necessary for their well-being. Advocacy can take many forms, from helping clients navigate complex healthcare systems to challenging systemic barriers that impact mental health. In some cases, this involves recognising when a client's needs extend beyond psychological therapy and referring them to appropriate services, such as medical professionals, social workers, or specialised support groups. By collaborating with other services, counselling psychologists help to create a more holistic support ecosystem (see Chapter 11), ensuring that clients receive comprehensive care.

For example, a counselling psychologist working with a client who is both vulnerably housed and struggling with severe anxiety may recognise that therapy alone is not enough to address their situation. Whilst helping the client manage their emotional distress, the psychologist may also advocate on their behalf by referring them to housing services, financial support programmes, etc. Over time, the psychologist might observe improvements not only in the client's emotional well-being but also in their ability to access stable accommodation and feel more secure in daily life. This example highlights how advocacy and referrals can work alongside therapy to support a client's overall well-being.

Before moving on to consider the impact that counselling psychologists can have upon services, as briefly referred to earlier, it is important to acknowledge that not all change resulting from the work that they engage with counselling psychologists in is necessarily positive. Whilst therapy is often associated with growth, healing, and transformation, the process can also be challenging, emotionally demanding, and, at

Iatrogenic effects are unintended negative consequences or harm caused by a treatment or intervention itself, rather than the original condition or difficulty.

times, even harmful. Some clients may experience distress, a worsening of symptoms, or feel misunderstood, invalidated, or be retraumatised within the therapeutic relationship. Furthermore, therapy, like all types of support, carries the potential for **iatrogenic effects**, where the intervention itself unintentionally causes harm. These outcomes may stem from mismatches in therapeutic approach, ruptures in the relationship that are not adequately repaired, or from systemic factors such as cultural insensitivity, power imbalances, or organisational pressures that compromise care. Recognising these realities is not about undermining the value of therapy, but about fostering a reflective, ethical stance that remains alert to the complexity and risk inherent in psychological work. Arguably, counselling psychologists, with their emphasis on critical reflexivity and depth of relating, are well positioned to hold space for this complexity and to strive towards practices that reduce harm and promote safe, collaborative, and culturally attuned support.

Reflexive activity: considering the impact of therapy on individuals

Think about a time when you faced a personal challenge or transition (e.g. academic stress, a relationship change, or a move to a new environment).

1 How did you navigate this experience? What helped you cope?
2 Imagine you had therapy during that time – what kind of support might have been helpful?
3 Reflect on the idea of the client as the 'hero' in therapy. How does this shape your view of the psychologist's role?
4 Write a short (150–200 word) reflection on what this exercise teaches you about the impact therapy might have upon on an individual.

Advocating for service level changes

Counselling psychologists' roles often involve contributing to conversations about the development of services. Whilst a lot of the work that they will do in the early stages of their career is with individuals, this often expands outwards to the environments and services in which they work.

As a consequence, they can become important advocates for service level changes. Whilst this will be more commonplace for those with service management or commissioning job roles that involve the oversight of involved in leadership roles (as outlined in chapter 5), it is not uncommon for all counselling psychologists to be involved in service development activities. Below we outline some of the activities that counselling psychologists might see themselves taking on.

Consultation and collaboration with colleagues

Counselling psychologists often engage in consultation and collaboration with colleagues and other professionals, such as social workers, psychiatrists, teachers, and healthcare providers. The role of the counselling psychologist in these collaborations might be to support the development of more holistic, client-focused services that consider the many different needs of service users. By sharing their psychological expertise, they can help to inform decision-making, contribute to multidisciplinary team discussions, and work towards creating integrated approaches to care. Effective collaboration also involves advocating for evidence-based practices which make use of a broad assessment of the relevant research, enhancing the understanding of mental health and well-being issues within teams, and promoting culturally sensitive practices. Through these collaborative efforts, counselling psychologists can influence the design and delivery of services to create more supportive, inclusive environments.

Developing training and continuing professional development (CPD) resources

A more specific form of consultancy might be the role that counselling psychologists take on when delivering training. Counselling psychologists play a valuable role in developing training and CPD opportunities within services, a role that can help to enhance the skills and knowledge of colleagues. Drawing on their psychological expertise, they can design and deliver training sessions on topics such as mental health awareness, trauma-informed pluralistic care, developing approaches to cultural humility or attunement, and research-informed interventions. By creating tailored CPD programmes, counselling psychologists have the opportunity to address the specific needs of multidisciplinary teams, ensuring that staff are best equipped to provide high-quality, client-focused care. In addition, counselling psychologists may support reflective practice and clinical supervision, fostering environments where learning and development are prioritised. As a consequence, their contributions to training and CPD not only support staff well-being and competence but also contribute to developing more effective and responsive services for clients.

Needs assessment and service evaluation

To contribute effectively to service-level changes, counselling psychologists can be involved in conducting needs assessments and evaluations to greater understand the experiences and challenges of service users. This can involve gathering feedback from those who have used the services on offer, sometimes referred to as **experts by experience**, through interviews, surveys, focus groups, or the use

> **Experts by experience** are individuals who use their lived experiences of mental health challenges or accessing therapeutic services to contribute to service development, research, and support initiatives.

of standardised assessment tools – many of the research skills developed whilst counselling psychologists are in training. By analysing this information, counselling psychologists can identify gaps in service provision, highlight areas that might benefit from improvement, and develop ways of working that are both research-informed and developed in collaboration with service users' feedback. Additionally, evaluating the impact of existing services can help to determine their effectiveness, information that can provide a foundation for advocating for specific changes going forward. This type of approach can help to ensure that service developments are grounded in real-world needs, rather than assumptions, and hopefully make improvements more relevant and impactful for those accessing support.

Designing and implementing interventions

In their efforts to improve services and fill gaps that might be identified in needs assessment processes, counselling psychologists often take on the role of designing and implementing interventions that address the specific needs of their client populations. These interventions might include developing psychoeducational workshops, creating support groups or developing specific therapeutic programmes for particular groups. In doing so, counselling psychologists will draw on their knowledge of psychological theories and evidence-based practices to tailor interventions that are the most likely to be effective, accessible, and culturally appropriate. In addition to this, they are likely to be involved in evaluating these interventions – again using their awareness of research methodologies – to ensure they achieve the desired outcomes and that they can make adjustments if needed. By designing thoughtful, client-focused support, counselling psychologists contribute to creating environments that support long-term well-being and recovery of those seeking support.

Engaging in advocacy and social justice work

Counselling psychologists are often driven by a commitment to social justice, seeking to address systemic inequalities that have negative impacts upon mental health and limit access to services. Their role in advocacy may involve raising awareness of marginalised or underserved communities, challenging discriminatory practices, and working towards the development of more inclusive policies. By using their psychological expertise to highlight the impact of social determinants of health – such as poverty, discrimination, or prior experiences of trauma – they can help to inform organisational changes that can promote fairness and accessibility. This is not always on a broader level, however, and individual therapeutic work can also be social justice informed by engaging with the political in our understandings of our clients' lives, engaging in collaboration and dialogue on our sociocultural identities and how they influence and interact with our experiences and relationships. On the level of individuals and services, counselling psychologists might also, for example, advocate on behalf of their clients by writing supportive letters regarding housing or benefits, or deliver training that builds cultural skills and humility within teams. In this way, counselling psychologists can work to create more inclusive and responsive mental health services.

Conclusion

The impact of counselling psychology extends across both individual and service levels, shaping not only the lives of clients but also the development of mental health and well-being services. As explored in previous sections, the work of counselling psychologists can influence individuals in multiple, interconnected ways – helping them to build self-awareness, develop emotional capacity and resilience, and foster personal growth. Importantly, these changes do not happen in isolation, often extending beyond the counselling psychologist's office and supporting individuals to learn about themselves and to develop skills to manage their well-being independently. In addition, at a service level, counselling psychologists contribute to shaping and improving mental health provisions through advocacy, training, and service development. Their work can help to ensure that therapeutic interventions remain accessible, effective, and responsive to the diverse needs of clients. Finally, therapy can create a ripple effect, not only benefiting individuals but also enhancing their relationships, workplaces, and communities. By working at both personal and systemic levels, counselling psychologists can help to create meaningful and lasting change that extends beyond the therapy room.

Reflexive questions

- Beyond symptom reduction, what are some of the ways that therapy can impact a client's life and how might these changes extend beyond the therapy room into their relationships, work, and overall well-being?
- How can outcome measures and feedback from clients be used to inform and improve mental health and well-being services?

Critical thinking questions

1 To what extent should therapy aim to challenge broader societal structures (e.g. discrimination, inequality) rather than focusing solely on individual change?
2 How can counselling psychologists ensure that service-level changes are evidence-based whilst also being responsive to the diverse needs of the individuals and communities they serve?

Further reading and resources

- **Routine Outcome Measures – https://www.bacp.co.uk/events-and-resources/research/routine-outcome-measures/**
  When considering whether counselling psychology services are having an impact on people's lives, it is important to be open and receptive to feedback from those using the service. Sometimes, due to the complex nature of the relationship, service users might not be able to verbalise their opinions freely. Many professional counselling and psychotherapy organisations therefore provide information on how to collate and report the impact that therapy can have upon people's lives using routine outcome measures. The *British Association for Counselling and Psychotherapy* has created these webpages as one such resource.
- **A toolkit for collecting routine outcome measures – https://www.bacp.co.uk/media/2355/bacp-cyp-prn-toolkit-for-collecting-routine-outcome-measures.pdf**
  This toolkit reflects upon the way that specific questionnaires might be used within work with children and young people to help demonstrate change. This includes reference to ways to encourage individuals to articulate their goals for therapy, tools to consider the quality of the therapeutic relationship, and measures of well-being.

- Impact toolkit for economic and social sciences – https:// www.ukri.org/councils/esrc/impact-toolkit-for-economic-and-social-sciences/
  Demonstrating the impact that counselling psychologists can have upon services is very complex. Resources such as those developed by research councils can provide thoughtful frames to make use of. This toolkit, developed by the *Economic and Social Research Council* in the UK, provides guidance on how to define impact and best practices for communicating with non-professional audiences.

References

Duncan, B. L., Miller, S. D., & Sparks, J. A. (2004). *The heroic client: A revolutionary way to improve effectiveness through client-directed, outcome-informed therapy,* Rev. ed (pp. xxi, 266). Jossey-Bass.

Parry, G. D., Crawford, M. J., & Duggan, C. (2016). Iatrogenic harm from psychological therapies – Time to move on. *The British Journal of Psychiatry, 208*(3), 210–212. https://doi.org/10.1192/bjp.bp.115.163618

Chapter 10

Impacting communities and policy

Introduction

Counselling psychologists are perhaps best known for working in psychological services: providing psychological assessment and interventions to individuals, families, or groups in mental health settings, in physical healthcare, education, or forensic settings, for example. This is often where we see our graduates go and work initially, beginning as newly qualified psychologists who do some assessment and therapeutic work, some supervision, or some service level work and development with and alongside other counselling psychologists and healthcare professionals. Much of this work is on a relatively small scale, however, serving individuals and groups, or service-users, carers, and families of the organisations we work with. By 'small', we do not mean in terms of significance, we mean to say that this work is closer to the individual within the systems we discussed in Chapter 4. This work, impacting individuals and services, is what we have described in Chapter 9, and we have discussed the important impact that counselling psychologists can potentially have on these levels.

Beyond this, however, counselling psychologists might have an influence on broader levels of intervention. By 'broader' we mean further out from the individual within those systems we introduced and located in Chapter 4, for example, further out towards our local communities, the media, and local and national government. In this chapter, we extend our gaze to consider some of this work. Often (though not always!), this is not where counselling psychologists begin their work, but it is an important part of what we can do, and therefore it is useful to consider what this might look like, and what skills we might use in these areas of our work. Many counselling psychologists will end up engaging in some or all of these ways of working during their careers. Like the introduction to Chapter 4, where we describe the way in which thinking about therapy and thinking about systems are not opposing, and are instead complementary and interrelated, our impacts on individuals, services,

DOI: 10.4324/9781003546733-15

communities, and policy are also interrelated. When we have an impact on individuals, we have an impact on the systems around them, and when we have an impact on communities and policy, we have an impact on individuals. What follows therefore is an unpacking of the possible settings and ways of working counselling psychologists might be situated within, which most directly impact on communities and policy.

Working in collaboration with community organisations

There are a variety of ways in which counselling psychologists might work with and alongside community organisations and groups to facilitate change. Importantly, this is not about counselling psychologists coming in to 'fix' things and bring their 'superior knowledge' to address the problems community groups are wrestling with (and then leaving). Consistent with the social justice principles outlined by Goodman et al. (2004), we want to ensure that communities have the tools they need going forward, rather than only being supported when we are there. Further, consistent with the idea of **epistemic justice** and other important principles of social justice action, counselling psychologists prize the knowledge and understanding of communities themselves, drawing on their own cultures and histories (Winter & Charura, 2023), rather than swooping in assuming they know best. Counselling psychologists might work alongside communities to support, learn, and address any difficulties or problems collaboratively. Thompson et al. (2024, pp. 254–279) outline ten key practice points for clinicians working in partnership with community organisations and include principles such as the need to:

- be open to organisational and cultural change and reflect on how their organisational cultures or practices might support or prevent community-driven work.
- identify and managing power relations appropriately.
- ensure all voices are heard and none monopolise.
- fully collaborate with community groups in all stages of the work, ensuring that the communities' needs and priorities are at the centre, and that accessibility is considered.

Epistemic justice relates to fairness in knowledge creation and communication, and a prizing of various sources and types of knowledge. Epistemic injustice occurs when some types of knowledge are ignored, unattributed, or dismissed.

- critically reflect on the purpose and focus of the work.
- have an open and transparent discussion regarding everyone's assumptions and expectations about the collaboration.
- agree on a plan for long-term sustainability.

Concrete examples of such work include counselling psychologists working alongside youth groups, charities, or organisations that support specific groups such as asylum seekers and refugees, or people who are experiencing homelessness. Or counselling psychologists might facilitate group dialogue between those with opposing views or those who are in conflict.

In Lunghy et al. (2023), the authors (including a psychologist, participatory action researchers, and youth worker) describe supporting a youth-led social action project 'Take Back the Power' and the **participatory action research** associated with this. In this, the psychologists and researchers involved worked alongside the young people (with lived experience of serious youth violence) to make decisions and act together, focusing on responses to serious youth violence and the broader connections with racism and inequalities. The process drew on different approaches, such as Street of Life (inspired by Ncazelo Ncube-Mlilo's Tree of Life: Ncube, 2006) where they considered aspects of their lives in a symbolic way, and reflective group activities such as 'The Wall of Injustice' where they mapped out their experiences together. Outputs included a Call to Action and a podcast, and they worked alongside MPs and other activists, as well as engaging in media work and broader campaigns. Counselling psychologists working on such community projects use their core relational skills working with group members, and communication skills as they engage with numerous different audiences and groups in different settings. We must also draw on our research and critical thinking skills, as well as our need to engage in reflective practice and be able to draw on our personal experiences, as well as navigate often quite complicated power relations, ensuring that we are working in ways which are consistent with our values. Principles of and ideas from social justice, intersectionality, and liberation psychology are therefore all useful to draw upon (see Chapter 2).

Other examples of working alongside community organisations can include supporting activist groups with the psychological side of

> **Participatory action research** is an approach to research and impact that involves working as collaborators with 'participants' or those involved in research from the outset and throughout the lifespan of the project.

their work or providing supervision to those who are in supportive (but not therapeutic) roles in community organisations. These roles may be more aligned with the impact on individuals and services we discussed in the previous chapter, but involve working with a wide range of organisations, not only those from psychological services and therapeutic settings. Supporting others to support others with

Experts by experience is one word used for people who contribute to mental health services by drawing on their own lived experience of mental health difficulties and using services. It is sometimes distinguished from 'experts by training', though this can create a false dichotomy, given that psychologists often have their own lived experience to draw on too. Other words used for experts by experience include survivors or people with lived experience.

the emotional labour they are doing in organisations which provide important community resources, or those which work with survivors or '**experts by experience**' can be a significant way for counselling psychologists to have a positive impact, as they support others and continue the important work of their organisations.

Working with media

One of the ways in which counselling psychologists might engage with broader communities and the public on a wider scale is through working with the media. This might include, for example, contributing to articles in the popular press or newspapers; or publishing self-help books or similar aimed at non-academic or non-psychology audiences; appearing on television or radio; blogging or vlogging; creating or featuring in podcasts; or influencing via social media on sites and apps such as Instagram, TikTok, BlueSky, Facebook, or X (formerly twitter). When working with printed press, television, or radio, counselling psychologists might contribute 'expert opinion', communicate findings from research projects, provide psychological advice or opinion to television producers, or provide psychological support for those appearing in reality television programmes, for example. Counselling psychologists might use social media to communicate psychological information and be an 'influencer' by creating and sharing content about their area of practice or research area, for example, sharing information about the psychological impacts of trauma or the difficulties parents experience post-birth. They might also use social media largely for business purposes, for example, to market their private practice work. Some research suggests that counselling psychologists might also use social media to contribute to social change and pursue particular issues connected to their social justice values, by contributing to campaigns or amplifying experiences or those who are marginalised (White & Hanley, 2025a).

This is obviously a sphere of work that takes us far away from the private and confidential nature of one-to-one therapeutic work, or even the work with communities described above. Work with the media potentially reaches a much greater audience and requires nuanced attention to the skills required and ethical responsibilities in this different medium. Kasket (2023) outlines the varying levels of control which psychologists might retain when working in these ways. High control situations are where you retain the majority or all the control over what is published and how, for example, when publishing a magazine or book where you have final approvals, or social media, which you largely curate. Medium control situations are where you might have a degree of control but not as much, for example, in live television interviews where the questioning might go in a different direction than expected, or pre-recorded segments where you don't have final approval on which segment of your talk will appear in the final versions. Finally, low control situations such as being interviewed by a journalist over the phone. In none of these scenarios, however, do you have complete control: even on social media, where you control the content, you do not have control over who re-posts your information out of context, or who comments on what you have shared. It's important to remember the way in which material published online has a permanence to it and can be shared very quickly across exceptionally wide people in different areas and geographies. Partly because of these issues, authors such as White and Hanley (2025b) have emphasised the importance of ethical principles specific to social media work in particular and the need to reflect on the management of ethical dilemmas related to confidentiality, risk management, and competence to work in these broader ways. Counselling psychologists can have a positive impact via working with the media, as they can reach a wider audience with important psychological information and work alongside others to create positive social change, but care and attention should be given to the ethical and social context of the work. Counselling psychologists can draw on their knowledge and expertise in this work and use their critical thinking and communication skills again. Communication in this format needs to be tailored to the audience and medium, for example, via thinking about what type of video or content people will best connect with, and how to ensure messages are clear and avoid ambiguity.

Reflexive activity: advocacy and visibility on social media

Many counselling psychologists use social media to raise awareness about mental health and well-being, share resources, or challenge stigma. Think about the role of social media in public education and advocacy. Consider:

- What are the potential benefits and risks of using social media for professional advocacy?
- How can counselling psychologists use these platforms ethically and effectively?
- What topics would you feel confident speaking about online?

Now write a short reflection (approximately 250 words) on how you might use social media as a tool for advocacy or public engagement.

Influencing policy

Another area where counselling psychologists might work and have an impact beyond their work with individuals and services is in relation to social policy. Increasingly, there is an emphasis on how practitioner psychologists might use their knowledge and expertise to inform the development of policy. Linking back to our earlier discussion of social justice, **policy advocacy** (working to inform and have an influence on policy) is one area where counselling psychologists might put their social justice values into action on a macro (or larger, perhaps even national) scale. Such work is often (but not always) supported by professional bodies such as the BPS and/or connected with research conducted in academic settings. For example, the BPS engages its members with consultations and briefings, noting that:

> Our consultations allow us to share the latest psychological evidence and support the development of well-informed policies. Our Parliamentary Briefings allow us to comment on government actions and decisions which affect our community.
>
> (*Consultations and Briefings*, n.d., page strap line)

At the time of writing, for example, counselling psychologists might wish to contribute to consultations

Policy advocacy involves aiming to contribute to and change social or public policy through influencing stakeholders and policymakers, often drawing on expertise from research or practice.

on the Welsh Government's 'All-Wales Perinatal Engagement Framework', updates to the 'Adults with Incapacity (Scotland) Act 2000' or a Scottish Government consultation on 'support available to young people as they leave

> **Policy briefing documents** are concise and focused documents for policy-makers, which outline evidence on an issue and the implications for policy, as well as proposed solutions.

care and enter adulthood'. Depending on a counselling psychologists' specific area of work, expertise and/or research knowledge they might feel able to contribute to such consultations, feeding in their psychological expertise and experience.

As well as responding to specific calls for contributions, as in the consultations described above, counselling psychologists might work to develop **policy briefing documents** in response to specific problems or policies. These would typically include an overview or introduction outlining the problem is and your (an individual or group of psychologists) relevant expertise, an overview of practice and research findings, and some concrete policy recommendations. O'Hare and Meheux (2023) describe their work in educational psychology, for example, on 'time to play' and 'catch up narratives'. Counselling psychologists can use these policy briefings to work to try and have a direct influence on policy advisors, civil servants, and MPs. Communication of key messages is important, and using various channels such as press and media work, social media, and networking with relevant stakeholders are all important strategies. Counselling psychologists who are based in academic institutions like universities might have Policy Teams they can work with, who will help with some of the arrangements with the media or communicating core messages.

Counselling psychologists do not enter the policy arena uncritically, however, and like all areas of the work, we would suggest that it is important to come back to our values, and our balancing of the reflective and scientist practitioner models. Some psychologists have urged caution in entering this territory. Walker and colleagues (2018), who focus on the connection between academic psychology research and the potential impact on social policy, argue that psychologists need to ensure they understand the complexity of the policy influence process, and remind us to consider the potential uses and misuses of our research when we publish it. They suggest that psychologists should ask ourselves what the implications of our work are for the communities we serve, rather than for policy, and perhaps that (although policy change might not necessarily follow) alliances of mental health service user groups and psychological researchers might actually have more real-world impact and might be 'a form of social activism' (p. 4).

When working to influence the development or change of social policy, counselling psychologists might draw upon many skills which are familiar to them in their psychological therapy-based work and perhaps some which extend those. These skills might include:

- Communication skills: being able to translate information and 'evidence' from practice and research into something understandable to those who are not from a psychology background
- Networking, relationship building and collaboration with a variety of people in different roles, in different organisations
- Self-care when engaging with policy in areas that directly impact you
- Taking a systems perspective
- Engaging in ongoing learning
- Managing pushback from people who disagree (Winter et al., 2024)

Conclusion

As can be seen in this chapter, counselling psychologists can occupy numerous roles and work at levels which move significantly beyond the one-to-one therapeutic work which dominates our training programmes. Working alongside and supporting communities, social organisations, and experts-by-experience allows counselling psychologists to take broader action and potentially have an influence in a different way. Working in the media, including social media, means that counselling psychologists can have a global impact in their work, and influencing policy can change how things work at national levels. In each of these different spheres, counselling psychologists might draw on not only their core relational, critical thinking, and research skills, but also utilise specific skills in communicating in different ways, networking and having a political influence, or thinking about ethical practice differently.

Reflexive questions

1 How comfortable would you feel with sharing information on social media platforms and being known publicly? How might you take care of yourself when engaging with this type of work?
2 How do you think your social and political identities influence the types of macro-level work you might be involved in as a counselling psychologist, and the ways in which you might work in these spaces?

Critical thinking questions

1 What do you think some of the reasons are for and against counselling psychologists having an influence on social policy?

2   How do you think that counselling psychologists can ensure that their work with community organisations is value-led and ensures a fair sharing of power?

Further reading and resources

- **Thompson, K., Tribe, R., & Zlotowitz, S. (2024). Guidance for clinicians on working in partnership with community organisations. In R. Tribe & D. Bhugra (Eds.),** *Social justice, social discrimination, and mental health: Theory, practice, and professional issues.* **Routledge.**
  This really useful chapter outlines ten key practice points for clinicians working in partnership with community organisations.
- **Using Psychology to make better policy – https://www.bps.org.uk/guideline/using-psychology-make-better-policy**
  A BPS report reflecting how psychologists can use their work to influence policy.
- **Guidance for giving written or oral evidence to a House of Commons select committee – https://www.parliament.uk/globalassets/documents/get-involved2/select-committees/guidance-for-giving-evidence-to-a-house-of-commons-select-committee.pdf**
  Guidance from the UK parliament on how to provide evidence to select committee calls for evidence.

References

BPS. (n.d.). *Consultations and briefings.* BPS. Retrieved 4 July 2025, from https://www.bps.org.uk/consultations-and-briefings

Goodman, L. A., Liang, B., Helms, J. E., Latta, R. E., Sparks, E., & Weintraub, S. R. (2004). Training counseling psychologists as social justice agents: Feminist and multicultural principles in action. *The Counseling Psychologist, 32*(6), 793–836. https://doi.org/10.1177/0011000004268802

Kasket, E. (2023). Working with the media. In T. Hanley & L. A. Winter (Eds.), *The Sage handbook of counselling and psychotherapy* (5th ed., pp. 587–592). Sage.

Lunghy, E., Zlotowitz, S., & Wallis, L. (2023). Critical community psychology and participatory action research. In L. A. Winter & D. Charura (Eds.), *The handbook of social justice in psychological therapies* (pp. 198–209). Sage.

Ncube, N. (2006). The tree of life project using narrative ideas in work with vulnerable children in Southern Africa. *International Journal of Narrative Therapy and Community Work, 1,* 3–16.

O'Hare, D., & Meheux, M. (2023). Influencing policy and socio-political change. In L. A. Winter & D. Charura (Eds.), *The handbook of social justice in psychological therapies.* (pp. 210–221). Sage.

Thompson, K., Tribe, R., & Zlotowitz, S. (2024). Guidance for clinicians on working in partnership with community organisations. In R. Tribe & D. Bhugra

(Eds.), *Social justice, social discrimination, and mental health: Theory, practice, and professional issues.* Routledge.

Walker, C., Speed, E., & Taggart, D. (2018). Turning psychology into policy: A case of square pegs and round holes? *Palgrave Communications, 4*(1), 108. https://doi.org/10.1057/s41599-018-0159-8

White, E., & Hanley, T. (2025a). 'I think that we can effect change': Psychologist use of social media for social justice advocacy. *Psychology and Psychotherapy: Theory, Research and Practice, 98*(4), 884–900. https://doi.org/10.1111/papt.12601

White, E., & Hanley, T. (2025b). "What I share is not the same as therapy": Psychologist experiences of Instagram use as a mental health influencer. *Psychology and Psychotherapy: Theory, Research and Practice, 98*(3), 624–642. https://doi.org/10.1111/papt.12585

Winter, L. A., & Charura, D. (2023). An introduction to the handbook of social justice in psychological therapies. In L. A. Winter & D. Charura (Eds.), *The handbook of social justice in psychological therapies: Power, politics, change* (pp. 3–9). Sage.

Winter, L. A., Wood, M., & Shriberg, D. (2024). Social justice and public policy: Learning from school and counseling psychologists. *School Psychology International, 45*(4), 337–358. https://doi.org/10.1177/01430343231201858

Part 5

Key emerging areas

In this section of the book, we take stock of the way that counselling psychology has already grown in the UK and reflect upon two areas of work that we believe require further attention going forward. These topics are by no means exhaustive or indeed exclusive, but reflect two areas that we believe are changing the landscape of counselling psychology going forward. It is also notable that, whilst the acknowledgement of their importance is somewhat emergent within the broad landscape of applied psychology within the UK, they are not new topics. Both chapters therefore reflect upon the ways in which counselling psychology as a discipline and counselling psychologists as professionals are embedding such thinking into their work.

- In Chapter 11, we start with the way in which counselling psychologists are increasingly taking on roles in which they work to provide support or enhance learning by orchestrating multiple resources. In doing so, they develop ecosystems of support that can be informed by humanistic psychological thinking. These purposefully attempt to mobilise different resources in between meetings with them and involve counselling psychologists working to influence systemic change, challenge fragmentation in care, and creatively integrate diverse sources of support (both formal and informal) around an individual's needs.
- In Chapter 12, we turn to the increasing commitment within the profession to anti-oppressive thinking and practices. As social justice and critical perspectives gain prominence in counselling psychology, this chapter explores how psychologists are engaging in sustained reflection and action to challenge systemic inequalities and oppressive structures within and beyond their work. It highlights the importance of 'becoming' anti-oppressive, acknowledging that this is a dynamic, evolving practice that requires humility, accountability, and a willingness to confront complicity and privilege.

DOI: 10.4324/9781003546733-16

Developing ecosystems of support and learning

Introduction

Throughout much of the history of therapy, a great deal of attention has been placed upon the time that an individual seeking support spends with a therapist. As discussed in Chapter 9, the therapist might often be viewed as the hero of the storyline of a therapy. This, however, is far from the reality of how therapy often unfolds. Typically, therapy might take the form of a weekly 50-minute session and, in the time in between, a great deal of work is engaged in by the client themselves. They apply new learning, try out new techniques, make use of new coping strategies, and consider the reflections they made in therapy to understand their emotions more in their day-to-day living. Whilst therapy sessions are commonly not an easy process for people to engage in, the process that follows might arguably be viewed as harder. Therefore, some counselling psychologists consider:

1 How it might be possible to recognise and mobilise more resources that can provide complementary support during these in-between periods.
2 Whether the typical therapeutic structure and traditions need to be challenged when working with some individuals to provide more fitting and holistic support for them.

As community interventions continue to grow, and new technologies are developed to support mental health and well-being, counselling psychologists are increasingly attempting to harness a variety of supportive resources in the roles that they take on. With this trend in mind, below we reflect upon the practice of recognising professional involvement within, or the orchestration of ecosystems (or an ecological system) of psychological support and learning. More specifically, we consider those that align with humanistic psychological and ecological theoretical thinking, theories that commonly underpin the work of counselling psychologists,

DOI: 10.4324/9781003546733-17

before describing a way of understanding the different elements that make up these systems. In the final sections we then discuss the involvement that counselling psychologists might have within them, the way in which these might be applied and provide some case studies to illustrate what these ecosystems might look like in real work contexts.

What is an ecosystem of psychological support and learning?

An ecosystem of psychological support and learning refers to the interconnected network of resources, relationships, and services that contribute to a person's psychological well-being at individual, community, and societal levels. Rather than existing as isolated interventions, psychological support operates within a broader system that includes naturally occurring support (such as friends, family, and peer networks), early intervention services, ongoing professional therapy, crisis response, and policy-driven initiatives. This multi-layered structure can help ensure that individuals have the opportunity to access appropriate support depending on the nature, immediacy, and severity of their psychological needs. By viewing psychological support as an ecosystem, we also acknowledge the dynamic interplay between personal characteristics, social connections, and formal mental health services in contributing to well-being outcomes.

Ecologically informed humanistic psychological interventions (i) hold the belief that individuals can constructively learn about themselves and grow if provided with the correct environment (notably one that is empathic, respectful and genuine) and (ii) recognise that individuals are embedded within complex social, cultural, and environmental systems that each influence the fertility of the context they are within (Hanley et al., 2020). Rooted in the principles of humanistic psychology described in Chapter 2 and informed by the systemic thinking described in Chapter 4, these approaches consider the person's internal world alongside their interactions with the broader contexts in which they live. Counselling psychologists working from this perspective aim to foster agency, connection, and meaning making by both attending to the individual and the environment that surrounds them. For example, this might include considering an individual's relationships, community engagement, access to broader resources, and cultural identities. Interventions may involve exploring the client's sense of place, belonging, and purpose, as well as advocating for social justice and structural change when environmental factors contribute to psychological distress. This humanistic-ecological stance moves beyond individual symptom reduction, promoting well-being through empowering individuals within their ecosystems and recognising the mutual influence between personal growth and societal conditions. Figure 11.1 reflects how humanistic psychological theory and

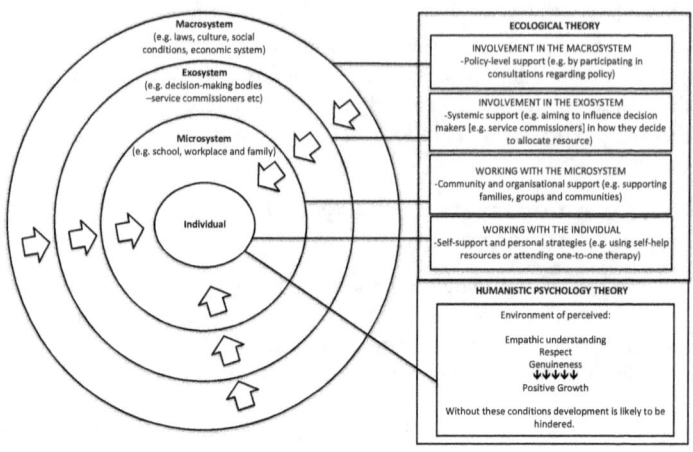

Figure 11.1 Ecologically informed humanistic psychology

ecological theory might be seen as working together. Further, the arrows within the figure also reflect the way that external pressures (e.g. from policy or organisations) can impact the layers that they envelop (e.g. communities, families, and individuals).

Before continuing, we should acknowledge that this idea is not a new one. Whilst therapeutic training has often prioritised relatively standard models of practice (e.g. individuals meeting in person for 50-minute sessions over a fixed number of weeks) some services have historically combined resources across sectors. For instance, there is much resonance with the concept of **psychologically informed environments** when supporting vulnerably housed individuals (Haigh et al., 2012) and the professions of youth work, education, and community development have all reflected upon holistic, systemically informed and responsive forms of support throughout their histories. Further, collective cultures, including those

Buen Vivir (Spanish for *'good living'* is a Latin American philosophy centred on collective well-being, community balance, and harmony with nature, rather than individual or material success.

Kapwa (Tagalog for *'shared self'*) is a Filipino Indigenous value that emphasises interconnectedness and seeing others as part of the self, recognising that identity is inherently relational.

informed by ideas such as **Ubuntu** rooted in the Bantu-speaking communities of Southern Africa, **Kapwa** in the Philippines, and **Buen Vivir** in parts of Latin America, have also emphasised the deep interconnection between individuals and their social, spiritual, and ecological environments. These traditions challenge individualistic assumptions and point towards more relational understandings of well-

> **Psychologically informed environments (PIE)** are spaces or services designed to take psychological and emotional needs into account, aiming to create supportive, trauma-aware conditions that promote well-being and positive relationships.
>
> **Ubuntu** is an African philosophy that emphasises shared humanity, stating that a person is a person through their relationships with others: *"I am because we are"*.

being. Such a view, whilst less well developed, is also evident in the writing of key humanistic psychologists such as Carl Rogers who made use of his therapeutic theory to consider the process of education (Rogers, 1969) and the role of politics for humanity and social change (Rogers, 1977). More specifically, ecological humanistic psychology, as discussed by Kuhn (2001), similarly calls for a shift beyond isolated individualistic models and towards approaches that integrate human experience within its broader environmental and cultural contexts. Together, these perspectives remind us that culturally and ecologically grounded approaches of counselling psychology are not innovations, but part of a longer, often overlooked, lineage of therapeutic thinking and practice.

Stratifying an ecosystem of psychological support and learning

As introduced, an ecosystem of psychological support and learning is a multi-layered system that integrates various forms of mental health and well-being activity. We all have these systems – they help shape who we are and influence how we are supported, or inhibited, in reaching our potential. Recognising this structure enables a more dynamic and inclusive view of mental health and well-being. It also allows for greater appreciation of both informal and formal contributions, and how personal experiences are often shaped by political and structural forces (see Chapter 2).

One way of understanding this ecosystem is through a continuum loosely inspired by Bronfenbrenner's (1979) ecological model – encompassing **microsystems, mesosystems, exosystems, macrosystems,** and **chronosystems.** Each layer plays a distinct role, and their true value often lies in how they interact with and reinforce one another. In practice, support aligned with this ecological view may range from self-directed strategies to broader systemic interventions. Below, we outline five types of support linked to these different layers. In reading on, it is important to acknowledge that these types do not map neatly onto Bronfenbrenner's levels – there is inevitable overlap, and many forms of support may function across layers. For instance, specialist services might provide support to individuals whilst also engaging with the systems they are embedded in, such as families, communities, or institutions. Alternatively, they might be focused upon these latter groups rather than solely individuals. Counselling Psychologists are therefore encouraged to reflect on these intersecting layers when considering well-being. A systemic, context-sensitive approach can

Chronosystems refer to the dimension of time in ecological systems theory, capturing how individuals and their environments change over time. This includes life transitions (like starting a new job or losing a loved one) and broader historical shifts (such as political change or technological advancement).

Exosystems are the broader social systems that indirectly influence the individual, like service commissioners or local government services.

Macrosystems are the wider cultural, societal, and ideological contexts that shape values, norms, and policies affecting all other systems.

Mesosystems are the connections and interactions between different microsystems, such as the relationship between a person's family and their school or workplace. These links can significantly influence well-being by shaping how different areas of a person's life reinforce or conflict with each other.

Microsystems are the immediate environments an individual directly interacts with, such as family, school, peers, and work.

help ensure that interventions are responsive not only to individual needs, but also to the broader environments that shape psychological experience.

Self-support and personal strategies

At the most immediate level are the internal resources people draw on to regulate emotion, manage stress, and maintain well-being. These might include practices such as journaling, exercise, breathing techniques, or the use of digital self-help tools. Increasingly, technology has expanded this layer through mobile apps, virtual mental health libraries, artificial intelligence resources and online well-being courses. Though often undervalued, this level can be empowering and preventative, especially when individuals feel resourced and informed.

Informal and social support networks

This layer includes the naturally occurring relationships and social ties that surround individuals. These include friends, family, neighbours, spiritual communities, and peer groups. These relationships offer things like emotional reassurance, companionship, and practical assistance. Support at this level is usually reciprocal, grounded in empathy and shared experience rather than formal expertise. For many, this is the first and most consistent form of care, especially during everyday difficulties or transitions.

Community and organisational support

Sitting between informal and formal care, this layer involves structured but often non-clinical interventions. These may include peer-led groups, school-based mental health programmes, workplace well-being initiatives, or community hubs offering safe spaces and signposting. The development of digital communities and moderated online peer forums has further expanded access to this layer. These services bridge gaps, reduce stigma, and increase psychological reach, especially for those who may not yet access, or even wish to avoid, more formal support.

Specialist and clinical services

Professional interventions form a more structured layer of support, typically offered in response to complex, persistent, or acute mental health and well-being challenges. These include therapeutic services, psychiatric care, and multidisciplinary teams in health and social care settings. Support at this level is informed by psychological theory, guided by ethical codes, and often delivered through integrated care pathways. Delivery may occur in-person, remotely, or through hybrid models, and may be offered by service in the public, private, or charitable sectors.

Systemic and policy-level support

The outermost layer consists of the social, economic, and political systems that influence how mental health and well-being support is conceptualised and resourced. Policies on healthcare funding, housing, education, and employment have direct and indirect impacts on mental well-being, both positive and negative. Equally, digital infrastructure, national mental health campaigns, and research-driven service design contribute to how care is organised and accessed. This layer often determines the availability and responsiveness of every other part of the system.

Reflexive activity: mapping your ecosystem of support

At this point we ask you to pause and create a map of your own ecosystem of support. Follow the instructions below and consider the various forms of support that contribute to your psychological well-being.

Instructions:

1 **Draw a map of your ecosystem of support**
    Place yourself at the centre of a page. Around you, map out the people, services, spaces, and structures that contribute to your well-being. These may include:

    - *Self-support and personal strategies:* personal coping strategies, beliefs, or habits
    - *Informal and social support networks:* friends, family, flatmates, pets
    - *Community and organisational support:* student societies, cultural groups, faith-based communities
    - *Specialist and clinical services:* university counselling, GP, helplines, academic tutors
    - *Systemic and policy-level support:* housing, financial aid, transport, academic policies

2 **Reflect**
After creating your map, take 10–15 minutes to consider:

    - Which forms of support do you currently rely on most?
    - Are there gaps or areas you'd like to strengthen?
    - How do these supports interact or overlap?
    - What does this map reveal about the ecosystem that supports your mental health and well-being?

Counselling psychologists and ecosystems of support and learning

Counselling psychologists regularly work within complex ecosystems of psychological support and learning. These ecosystems are incredibly varied and include informal social networks, professional services, community-based initiatives, and structural supports. Rather than working in isolation, counselling psychologists frequently collaborate across these levels, sometimes providing direct care, other times consulting, coordinating, or contributing to systemic change. Their work is shaped by a commitment to relational, individual-focused, and contextually aware practice, which allows them to meet clients where they are, psychologically, socially, and culturally. Below we outline some of the ways that counselling psychologists might offer support.

Therapeutic interventions

Central to the work of counselling psychologists is the delivery of psychological therapy. Counselling psychologists offer short-term, structured interventions for specific issues, as well as long-term, exploratory therapy for more complex or enduring difficulties. Making use of a pluralistic foundation, they adapt therapeutic approaches to suit the client's needs and circumstances. Increasingly, therapy may be delivered in hybrid or fully digital formats, including video sessions, secure messaging platforms, or therapy-assisted apps, enhancing accessibility for individuals who might struggle to access in-person care.

Psychoeducation and preventative support

Counselling psychologists also engage in psychoeducation, helping individuals and groups to better understand emotional well-being, psychological processes, and coping strategies. This might take the form of workshops that focus upon topics such as managing anxiety, online resources for learning about emotional regulation, or digital modules promoting self-care strategies. By promoting mental health literacy, psychoeducation can act as a key preventative layer within the ecosystem of support, empowering individuals before more intensive interventions are required.

Consultation and collaborative practice

Another critical function is consultation. Counselling psychologists often work alongside other professionals, such as educators, doctors, social workers, and organisational leaders, to offer psychological insight that enhances the support available within those systems. This could include advising on workplace mental health policy, co-developing student support frameworks, or offering reflective practice groups for frontline staff. Digital tools may also be used here, such as outcome monitoring platforms and shared care records, enabling joined-up approaches to care.

Service and policy development

At a systemic level, counselling psychologists contribute to the planning, delivery, and evaluation of mental health services. This may involve conducting research, developing new clinical pathways, supporting training initiatives, or influencing policy decisions at institutional or national levels. Technology is often a part of this work, whether through digital mental health service design, app-based interventions, or the use of digital approaches of support to bridge geographical gaps in care provision.

Community engagement and social justice practices

Rooted in a commitment to ethical and socially responsive practice, counselling psychologists often engage in community-based work and social justice initiatives. This may include outreach to underserved populations, developing culturally appropriate interventions, or campaigning for greater equity in mental health services. Technological tools, such as social media campaigns or the development of freely available community resource platforms, can also play a role in amplifying voices and increasing reach.

A note on the use of technology within an ecosystem of support and learning

Counselling psychologists may actively advocate for the thoughtful integration of technology as a means of enhancing accessibility, continuity, and personalisation within psychological support ecosystems. This is a trend that has certainly increased since the Covid-19 pandemic (Hanley, 2021). Rather than viewing digital tools as replacements for human connection however, they often promote their use as complementary resources that can extend the reach and flexibility of care. This might include recommending evidence-based well-being apps, supporting clients in accessing online psychoeducation, or offering therapy through secure digital platforms. In contexts where traditional services are difficult to access, such as rural areas, marginalised communities, or during times of crisis, technology can help bridge gaps and reduce barriers to access.

Importantly, counselling psychologists also critically engage with the ethical, environmental, and relational dimensions of digital tools. This includes recognising the digital divide, the potential for data misuse or surveillance, and the risk of depersonalisation in therapeutic relationships. They may also reflect on the environmental impact of digital infrastructures and the extractive practices underpinning the development of certain technologies. Ensuring that digital technologies are used in ways that align with individual needs, therapeutic goals, and values of inclusivity, empowerment, and ecological responsibility is therefore vital. In this way, counselling psychologists can contribute to the development of more adaptive, just, and sustainable mental health and well-being ecosystems that harness both human connection and digital innovation.

Orchestrating and co-ordinating ecosystems of support and learning

Counselling psychologists are well positioned to work across the layers of psychological support, not only providing therapeutic interventions but also orchestrating and co-ordinating broader systems of care. Their work is informed by a relational and context-sensitive perspective that recognises mental health is shaped by multiple, interacting influences. Rather than focusing solely on individual change, counselling psychologists who aim to create ecosystems of support help individuals navigate, access, and build supportive networks that reflect their unique needs and circumstances. This is closely aligned with pluralistic approaches to therapy (see Chapter 2), which emphasise tailoring support and recognising that meaningful change often takes place both within and beyond the therapy room. This work calls for a deep sense of humility, acknowledging that no single practitioner, type of professional or therapeutic model holds all the answers, and that effective support often emerges through collaboration, co-construction, and listening.

At the core of this process is the ability to map the support landscape around an individual. This involves exploring existing relationships, personal coping strategies, and formal or informal sources of support. By understanding what is already in place, and where there are gaps, a counselling psychologist can help to strengthen underused resources whilst sensitively addressing areas of unmet need. This mapping is not only practical but can also be empowering, as it encourages clients to take ownership of their mental health and well-being journey within the context of their lives.

Orchestrating support can also involve layering and sequencing interventions over time. A client may initially require short-term therapy to address immediate distress, followed by opportunities for longer-term relational work or reintegration into peer networks, community groups, or meaningful activities. Counselling psychologists are trained to think ecologically about these transitions, matching interventions to current needs whilst planning for sustainable, holistic support. Technology increasingly plays a role in this process, offering accessible tools such as self-help apps, online psychoeducation, or mediated check-ins that can complement in-person care.

In many contexts, counselling psychologists act as bridges between services and systems. They may liaise with doctors, educators, mental health teams, or social care professionals to ensure that care is joined up and consistent. This role is especially vital in settings such as the NHS, schools, universities, or third-sector organisations, where service users often encounter fragmented care that is not always well joined up. Orchestration here involves helping clients navigate complex systems, advocating on their behalf when needed, and contributing to the creation of more responsive and person-focused care pathways. Importantly, these relational efforts require a willingness to engage with difference, negotiate shared understandings, and remain open to others' expertise.

Beyond the individual level, counselling psychologists aim to contribute to shaping the ecosystem itself. Through consultation, service design, and research, they engage with systemic and structural concerns, such as improving access to services, developing inclusive practices, or co-producing resources with service users. These contributions are essential to ensuring that ecosystems of support remain flexible, culturally responsive, and ethically grounded. In doing so, counselling psychologists play a role not only in individual change but also in shaping the conditions that make well-being more attainable across a diverse range of communities.

Crucially, whilst counselling psychologists may engage at multiple levels of care, they also recognise their limits and scope. In some contexts, their role may focus solely on offering therapy and developing therapeutic relationships. In other contexts, they may take on more expansive coordinating functions, helping individuals to access or make sense of wider support networks. Their ability to shift between these roles, guided by reflexivity, respect, and relational sensitivity, is part of what we believe makes a counselling psychologist's contribution different to many other therapeutic professions.

Ultimately, orchestrating an ecosystem of psychological support is not simply about assembling resources; it is about attuning to context, building trust, and enabling choice. The counselling psychologist's role is both strategic and relational, grounded in humanistic values and a commitment to supporting well-being in its fullest, most interconnected sense.

Case studies: ecosystems of support and learning in UK counselling psychology practice

Counselling psychologists in the UK are increasingly working within ecosystemic frameworks that acknowledge the interplay between individual psychological needs and wider social, relational, and structural factors. Below are two case examples, one from a university setting and one within the NHS Talking Therapies programme. Both aim to demonstrate how integrated, multi-modal support systems can be co-ordinated to meet clients' diverse needs.

Case 1: university-based ecosystem for a student with complex needs

Sophie, a 23-year-old university student, was referred to a counselling psychologist via student well-being services after reporting symptoms of anxiety, low mood, and academic disengagement. Her difficulties were compounded by a recent bereavement, a history of early trauma, and identity-related concerns. A thorough assessment, considering biopsychosocial elements, revealed a combination of internal and external stressors, including financial insecurity, social isolation, and a strained family environment.

The counselling psychologist adopted a relational and trauma-informed approach, embedding individual therapy within a wider network of support. Weekly in-person therapy drew from integrative models, including compassion-focused and cognitive-behavioural strategies, to help Sophie process loss and rebuild some sense of control over her day-to-day life. Recognising the impact of contextual factors, the psychologist liaised with academic support services to secure deadline extensions and a reduced workload. Sophie was also referred to a student-led peer support group to reduce isolation and enhance her social connectedness.

To address financial and housing instability, at Sophie's request, the psychologist contacted and collaborated with a local charity providing welfare advice and practical support. Additionally, Sophie was linked to a GP through the university health service to explore medication for sleep and appetite issues. Over nine months, this ecosystem of formal and informal interventions enabled Sophie to regain a sense of agency, re-engage academically, and develop healthier relational patterns.

Case 2: hybrid care in NHS talking therapies for a client facing a life transition

Amir, a 28-year-old client, accessed an NHS Talking Therapies service via his GP after relocating to a new city for work. He presented with symptoms of depression, emotional numbness, and low motivation. An ecologically informed humanistic assessment revealed deeper issues related to early relationships with caregivers, a lack of community ties, and work-related stress.

The counselling psychologist designed an intervention plan that combined digital and in-person support. Amir was initially introduced to an NHS-endorsed mental health app offering guided cognitive-behavioural tools, mood tracking, and mindfulness exercises. This supported self-regulation and the development of emotional insight whilst he awaited therapy.

Once therapy began, Amir attended weekly in-person sessions grounded in compassion-focused and person-centred approaches. Sessions focused on building self-compassion, addressing long-standing self-critical beliefs, and exploring interpersonal challenges. In parallel, Amir joined a six-week online psychoeducational group within the service, exploring emotional resilience, stress management, and values-based living alongside peers.

To strengthen Amir's local support network, the psychologist liaised with his GP and a social prescriber, who connected him to a men's well-being group and local volunteering opportunities. With Amir's consent, the psychologist also collaborated with his workplace well-being lead to explore strategies for managing workload and reducing stress. The integration of digital tools, therapeutic relationships, and community-based resources supported Amir's recovery and contributed to long-term well-being.

Reflections on ecosystemic practice

In both of the cases reported here, counselling psychologists moved beyond isolated individual interventions, facilitating multi-layered ecosystems of support that combined personal, relational, and environmental resources. Whilst Sophie's case highlights how educational and social structures can be integrated into psychological care, Amir's example demonstrates the potential of combining technology, in-person therapy, and social prescribing within NHS primary care. These humanistic interventions are ecologically informed, viewing individuals as embedded within systems of meaning, community, and power. Rather than focusing solely on symptom reduction, these approaches aim to enhance personal agency, strengthen naturally occurring support networks, and promote well-being within real-world contexts. Further, by working collaboratively with other professionals, using technology creatively, and advocating for system-level change, counselling psychologists are well-positioned to offer integrative, responsive care that meets people where they are, both psychologically and socially.

Conclusion

Counselling psychologists who advocate for the development of ecosystems of psychological care believe that improvements in well-being are not typically achieved through isolated interventions. Instead, they see well-being as a process that is a response to numerous interconnected layers of support, including personal, informal and social, community and organisational, and systemic and policy-level domains. Counselling psychologists can play a vital role within this structure, offering specialist psychological interventions whilst also supporting individuals to navigate and build upon the resources around them. Whether working one-to-one, with groups, consulting across services, or contributing to policy and service development, counselling psychologists can bring a holistic, relational lens that honours complexity and context.

Technology, cultural awareness, and systemic collaboration increasingly shape the way care is delivered and received. Further, no single professional or approach can meet the full range of mental health and well-being needs. This perspective reinforces the sentiment that professionals are stronger together, and we believe that working in this way can be hugely beneficial to those seeking support. Working within an ecosystem does however require humility, shared responsibility, and a willingness to collaborate across disciplines and communities. It invites counselling psychologists to remain reflexive, to champion inclusivity, and to hold both the individual and the system they are embedded within in mind. As we move towards more integrated and adaptive models of care, counselling psychologists with their pluralistic outlook are well placed to help shape ecosystems that are not only effective but also ethical, compassionate, and sustainable.

Reflexive questions

1 How do you feel about the idea of a counselling psychologists' role being to orchestrate an ecosystem of psychological support and learning? Does this excite, challenge, or unsettle you in any way?

2 How might you respond, internally or emotionally, when you notice systemic barriers that contribute to a client's distress? How might this response shape the way that you work with the individual or the broader systems that they inhabit?

Critical thinking questions

1 How do counselling psychologists navigate the tension between working relationally with individuals and influencing systemic or policy change? Is it possible to do both effectively, or are compromises inevitable?

2 What role does technology play in expanding or restricting access to support? Are digital mental health tools empowering, or do they risk depersonalising care or excluding those without digital access?

Further reading and resources

• **The Hub of Hope** – https://hubofhope.co.uk/
   This is a directory of mental health services based in the United Kingdom. It is a useful resource for finding resources in geographical regions that might help to develop an ecosystem of support.

- Kuhn, J. L. (2001). Toward an ecological humanistic psychology. *Journal of Humanistic Psychology, 41*(2), 9–24. https://doi. org/10.1177/0022167801412003
  This paper argues for a humanistic psychology that acknowledges individuals as part of interrelated systems (social, cultural, and ecological). The paper situates well-being within larger environmental and relational contexts.
- Hanley, T., Winter, L. A., & Burrell, K. (2020). Supporting emotional well-being in schools in the context of austerity: An ecologically informed humanistic perspective. *British Journal of Educational Psychology, 90*(1), 1–18. https://doi.org/10.1111/bjep.12275
  This paper reflects upon the way that social policy can ripple down to directly impact upon the lives and well-being of individuals.

References

Bronfenbrenner, U. (1979). *The ecology of human development: Experiments by nature and design.* Harvard University Press.

Haigh, R., Harrison, T., Johnson, R., Paget, S., & Williams, S. (2012). Psychologically informed environments and the "Enabling Environments" initiative. *Housing, Care and Support, 15*(1), 34–42. https://doi.org/10.1108/14608791211238412

Hanley, T. (2021). Researching online counselling and psychotherapy: The past, the present and the future. *Counselling and Psychotherapy Research, 21*(3), 493–497. https://doi.org/10/gk87gz

Hanley, T., Winter, L. A., & Burrell, K. (2020). Supporting emotional well-being in schools in the context of austerity: An ecologically informed humanistic perspective. *British Journal of Educational Psychology, 90*(1), 1–18. https://doi.org/10.1111/bjep.12275

Kuhn, J. L. (2001). Toward an ecological humanistic psychology. *Journal of Humanistic Psychology, 41*(2), 9–24. https://doi.org/10.1177/0022167801412003

Rogers, C. R. (1969). *Freedom to learn.* Charles E. Merrill Publishing.

Rogers, C. R. (1977). *On personal power.* Delacorte Press.

Chapter 12

Increasing anti-oppressive practices

Introduction

...being inclusive means to 'other' minoritized communities and groups, while taking up a position yourself as 'normative' and allowing the 'normative' identity to stay invisible. Being inclusive means to include those who are oppressed but still maintain your power by positioning yourself as normative, neutral, centred and invisible. Inclusive implies that there must be a level of exclusion taking place ... Anti-oppressive practice explicitly acknowledges structural and systemic inequalities, systems of oppression and the entire power-oppression relational dynamic ... Anti-oppressive practice not only acknowledges systemic and structural inequalities but intentionally works to flatten the power in therapeutic practice, processes, and relationships, to hold the client in equal regard to the practitioner and to prevent the client from being marginalized, minoritized or 'othered'.

(Khan, 2023, p. 29)

In earlier chapters, we have introduced you to the idea that counselling psychology embraces social justice values and practices, and we have considered various ways in which this might come into our practice. In this chapter, we build on this and look more closely at the idea of **anti-oppressive practice**.

> **Anti-oppressive practice** involves acknowledging systemic and structural inequalities and intentionally working to flatten the power in therapeutic practice, processes, and relationships. It also means holding the client in equal regard to the practitioner and to prevent the client from being marginalised, minoritised, or 'othered'.

DOI: 10.4324/9781003546733-18

Within this, we look to the future of counselling psychology and highlight the ways in which our profession can do better and build on progress in this area so far.

> **Social justice** is both a goal and a process which broadly relates to things like equality, anti-oppressive practices, fairness, inclusion, and shared decision-making.

We adopt the definition from Myira Khan presented above, which positions 'anti-oppressive' usefully in relation to ideas of inclusion, which have tended to dominate previous conversations about equality in psychological therapies, but which are rooted in problematic understandings of 'difference' that are othering, and do not disrupt unequal power relations. In this chapter, we take a forward-looking approach to consider how we can become more anti-oppressive in our work in years to come, and the areas in which we can become bolder and do better. Within this, we hold in mind the idea of **social justice** as ethical, reflexive, and politically informed when we consider what becoming anti-oppressive looks like (Winter & Charura, 2023).

First, though, it's perhaps important to ask: can counselling psychology truly be anti-oppressive? Throughout this chapter, we hope to emphasise our view that this is best thought of as a process counselling psychology 'becoming' rather than 'being': an understanding which recognises the importance of ongoing learning, growth and **cultural humility**, rather than about the profession being able to tick 'be anti-oppressive' off our to-do list. As Layla Saad wrote in her 2020 text *Me and White Supremacy*:

> I want to remind you that we are not looking for the happy ending, the teachable moment, or the pretty bow at the end of all the learning. We are also not looking for dramatic admissions of guilt or becoming so frozen with shame that you cannot move forward. The aim of this work is not self-loathing. The aim of this work is truth – seeing it, owning it, and figuring out what to do with it. This is lifelong work. Avoid the shortcuts, and be wary of the easy answers
>
> (Saad, 2020, p. 74)

This quote and the idea of a 'process of becoming' anti-oppressive are not only relevant to those who benefit from greater socially structured advantages and privileges (though perhaps most important to those who do). Second, as discussed in Chapter 4, intersectionality highlights the ways in which our privileged and oppressed identities intersect to influence our experiences. All of us have ways in which we can work to become bolder and to disrupt traditional power relations in our societies and in our field.

Can any applied psychology be truly anti-oppressive?

Psychology and the psychological professions have a very problematic history when we look at it through the lens of anti-oppressive practice. Instead of intentionally working to flatten power dynamics in therapeutic practices and relationships, or aiming to prevent people from being marginalised, minoritised, or 'othered' as in Khan's description of anti-oppressive practice above, psychological researchers and practitioners have been complicit in systems of oppression for many years. For example, psychological research and practice has contributed to the conception and perpetuation of systemic racism (Auguste et al., 2023); the oppression of disabled individuals is experienced within the counselling space (Reeve, 2000) and racially minoritised women's experiences were ignored as research and writing on women and mental health began to develop, thus centring white women as the 'presumed norm' (Burman et al., 1998, p. 234).

Alongside this there is, however, a longstanding commitment to becoming anti-oppressive and to social justice which should not be forgotten, with numerous textbooks and articles written over the years which describe anti-oppressive theories and practices within counselling psychology and allied fields (Brown, 2019; Lago & Smith, 2010; Parker, 1999; Pilgrim, 1997; Toporek et al., 2006; Tribe & Bhugra, 2025) This is not something new, though it has gained traction and become more commonly spoken of in recent years (which is not exclusively something to celebrate, as this process of popularisation sometimes dilutes radical thinking). This literature has repeatedly evidenced the way in which (as discussed in Chapter 4) we cannot remove the people we work with from society and the systems in which they are embedded within. Authors have demonstrated that practitioners focusing on well-being and mental health in their work must also be concerned with social identities, oppression, discrimination, and inequalities.

Individual and systemic barriers make becoming anti-oppressive on a larger scale in counselling psychology and other branches of psychology challenging. Challenges and barriers to engagement in social justice action, such as working in medically dominated contexts and the need for practitioners to be taken 'seriously', how one can bring together more traditional models of counselling with ideas of social justice, and available time for engaging in social justice action (Winter & Hanley, 2015) have been identified in the research literature. A lack of focus on social justice within clinical training environments can also be experienced as a barrier (Beer et al., 2012; Winter et al., 2025). Bemak and Chung (2008) speak of some of the personal barriers, including fear of being disliked or professionally ostracised if taking a different role which does not conform with typical expectations of a professional; being labelled as a troublemaker for promoting social justice values and advocacy; becoming complacent or apathetic when facing conflict with those who don't agree with a social justice approach; anxiety leading to guilt and inaction; and a false sense of powerlessness. Despite these barriers, we think it's by no means impossible for counselling psychology and counselling psychologists to become more anti-oppressive, and we have seen moves in that direction already: with increased research and professional articles written on topics such as anti-racism in psychology, challenging barriers to accessing services, supporting asylum seekers and refugees, and ensuring our services are inclusive for trans, non-binary, and gender diverse service users and carers. We have also seen an increase in training offered on things like equality, diversity, inclusion, and social justice (and a shift away from othering language in training e.g. 'working with diversity and difference'). Whilst these changes do not by themselves ensure we become more anti-oppressive in practice, they can all be seen as steps in the right direction.

The first step in increasing our anti-oppressive practice involves pausing and recognising the ways in which we are, both individually and collectively, complicit in systems of oppression (no matter who we are). This is an unpleasant and challenging ask and one which can lead to inaction, guilt, shame, and re-centring of privilege, which does not help us to move forward. We therefore must acknowledge this complicity alongside our commitment to action and to becoming bolder in our response to the problems around us.

We now shift our attention to the future of anti-oppressive practice in counselling psychology, and in the sections which follow, we look at the idea of 'becoming' anti-oppressive in more depth. We explore some areas in which we suggest counselling psychology and counselling psychologists can commit to becoming bolder over the years to come. As the forensic psychologist Seyed (Mehdi) Alemohammad, recently said: "We have the tools. We have the insight. What we need now is the courage. Let us be bold. Let us be loud. Let's be angry together" (Alemohammad, 2025, no page).

Reflexive activity: structural advantages and barriers

To help you think about how larger social systems impact who becomes a counselling psychologist and how they practice, take a few minutes to think about and answer the questions below. If you would like to, keep a record of your answers.

Your path into psychology

- What parts of your background (e.g. education, family support, language, money, identity) have helped you study psychology?
- Have you faced any challenges or barriers in getting to this point?

Who gets in and who is left out?

- Who do you think finds it easier to get on a training programme in counselling psychology in the UK?
- Who might find it harder, and why?

Looking forward

- How might these advantages or barriers impact how someone works as a psychologist?
- Why is it important for counselling psychologists to be aware of these issues?

The anti-oppressive journey in counselling psychology: a process of becoming

Carl Rogers wrote about 'becoming' a person, emphasising the human tendency towards growth and ongoing development. We argue that counselling psychology cannot simply 'be' anti-oppressive, and we will more than likely never be able to conclude that, nor should we wish to. Instead, the profession must commit to *ongoing* learning and development about issues of social justice, inequality, and oppression, in order that we remain open to and aware of the socio-political issues around us, our clients, and our relationships, and able to identify ways in which we can contribute to anti-oppressive practices. This idea mirrors the distinction we can see between **cultural competence** and **cultural humility**, which authors in psychology have written about. These are not complete opposites but are useful to contrast to illustrate the point we make about 'becoming' anti-oppressive.

Cultural competence requires psychologists to be competent, and to have certain awareness, knowledge, and skills which allow them to work transculturally.

A cultural competence approach requires psychologists to be competent and to have certain awareness, knowledge, and skills which allow them to work transculturally. This might include for example having an awareness of stereotypes and of their own background and biases; a knowledge of racial identity development, minoritised family structures, immigration, the effects of institutional barriers, "culture-bound, class-bound and linguistic features of psycholog-

Cultural humility is an approach in which individuals maintain an ongoing openness to learning about other cultures, recognise and challenge their own biases and assumptions, and prioritise respectful, collaborative relationships rather than assuming expertise over another's cultural experience.

Epistemic justice refers to fairness in knowledge production, sharing, and recognising. For us to have epistemic justice we should value differing types of knowledge and ways of understanding the world.

ical help"; and having skills in cultural aspects of assessment, a familiarity with research on racial groups, and is involved with minority groups outside of work (Sue, 2001, p. 799). The cultural competence model, inadvertently perhaps, implies an endpoint where you are 'competent', if you have ticked all the necessary boxes. **Cultural humility** in contrast places less emphasis on knowledge and achieving 'competence', and more on the need for critical self-examination and self-awareness, dialogue, and navigating cultural ruptures (e.g. a breakdown) in the therapeutic relationship (Mosher et al., 2017). Humility is an attitude that requires an openness to the other, a lifelong commitment to learning and growth, and a greater awareness of one's limitations. It requires us to remember that our knowledge, beliefs, values, and worldview are not superior to those of others. It therefore means we need to shift towards a valuing of different sources and frameworks of knowledge and understanding of the world and commit to **epistemic justice** in our work.

If we apply these ideas to counselling psychology and increasing anti-oppressive practice, we suggest that the field should commit to being humble and developing an attitude that we will never be done with this work. We make mistakes, we learn, and we grow. It is a process of 'becoming' rather than an aim to 'be'. In the next part of this chapter, we reflect on three example areas in which we think we need to become bolder on and which we might contribute to. Whilst counselling psychology has made significant strides in social justice and anti-oppressive practice in recent years there is a risk that the translation of values into action stops when people think that social justice is simply a part of counselling psychology. Social justice and anti-oppressive practices cannot just 'be', ticked off, complete, job done – they require ongoing reflection and action, and we must continue to become bolder over the years to come.

Counselling psychology and becoming bolder on

Decolonisation and anti-racism

In recent years, the discussion of anti-racism and decolonisation in counselling psychology and allied disciplines has increased significantly. This has been largely since the murder of George Floyd, a Black man in Minneapolis, USA, in May 2020, by a white police officer. This was one of many deaths of Black people at the hands of law enforcement and was followed by global Black Lives Matter protests. These events drew renewed attention to structural racism and violence against those who are racially minoritised. We then saw heightened attention on, for example, racial health inequities during the Covid-19 pandemic and beyond. The increase in attention and statements related to anti-racism has been critiqued by some for being tokenistic or performative, and arguably much of this is not enough and far too late. Nevertheless, the increased discussion and attention paid to research, writing, and experiences of racially minoritised psychologists and clients has undoubtedly had an important impact on counselling psychology, ensuring that attention is paid to the structures of racism, rather than considering racism as something which occurs on an individual level alone. Significantly, the American Psychological Association issued a formal apology to people of colour for their "Role in Promoting, Perpetuating, and Failing to Challenge Racism, Racial Discrimination, and Human Hierarchy in U.S." (APA, 2021). Looking forward, counselling psychology must ensure that the profession continues to do better, become bolder on tackling racism. Research continues to evidence time after time the impacts of systemic racism, and increased attention has been paid to evidencing the way in which this comes into clinical work, therapeutic training, and mental health more broadly. We must continue to challenge oppressive structures of racism, to publicly challenge political decisions which support supremacy, and instead to turn towards a decolonised approach to our discipline and work (see Turner, 2021, 2023, 2025).

Climate and ecological crises

We have seen a growing increase in a focus in psychology on climate and ecological crises, with writing and research concerned with 'eco anxiety' and climate-related distress becoming more common as we see more people presenting in therapy talking to us about their experience of climate change. The climate and ecological crises are not apolitical though and as with any other case of distress, we should not neglect a consideration of the socio-political context and systems (Klein, 2014). Oxfam reported that the richest 1% of the world's population were "responsible for 16% of global carbon emissions, which is the same as the emissions of the poorest 66% of humanity (5 billion people)" (Khalfan et al., 2023, p. x).

Milton (2023) summarises the way in which climate change is relevant to counsellors and psychologists: the direct influence it has on our mental health when our homes are flooded, or local areas are destroyed by wildfire, and the indirect influence via the impact of news and images of how others are directly impacted by climate change. Whether it is reported as such, climate change–related events are happening daily, both near and far. *Everyone* globally is impacted by this now (though those in the Global South are shouldering the greatest burden of impact), and this will only increase over years to come. As Milton notes: "People exist in time, responding both to events that *have* happened and alsoto our awareness of what *may* happen" (p. 40). For a number of years, psychologists focused their attention on how we can contribute to efforts to mitigate climate change by looking at how individuals make decisions about their own life choices and carbon footprint. Increasingly we are looking at how we can directly support those whose well-being and mental health are impacted by climate change. But counselling psychologists are also engaged in action which considers the broader political and social justice elements: challenging oil companies and those in positions of power and who hold great wealth and resources (e.g., the psychologists community group of Extinction Rebellion). This increasing emphasis on considering how humans relate to and are impacted by the natural world, and the focus on climate-related distress is welcome. To become bolder and do better, counselling psychologists can continue to extend our consideration of climate and ecological crises as political issues, which require a systemic understanding, rather than individual issues outside of such contexts.

'Culture wars' and divided societies

In the UK in recent years, we have seen increasing references made to 'culture wars' in society: hot topics where competing visions or moral/political views come into conflict (see Farrar & Hanley, 2023). Indeed, more broadly, political polarisation and stark differences in opinions and positionings between different groups of society have been increasingly highlighted in mainstream media, commentary, and debate. We have seen talk of various 'issues' coming under scrutiny, which often come down to social justice and matters of individual rights and freedoms of those who are or who have been marginalised or oppressed. For example (but not limited to) 'issues' of net zero (discussed above) are contested, the rights of trans, gender fluid, and non-binary people to live as they wish and to use the facilities they wish, the rights and conditions of living for those with refugee or asylum seeker status, and the responsibilities of the welfare state in relation to those who are disabled or in need of ongoing support.

Importantly, counselling psychology itself is not undivided on these issues, and is a profession made up of individuals with various political allegiances, beliefs, and positionings. When we (ourselves included) foreground the way in which counselling psychology has increasingly emphasised social justice, there are risks that some understand this as meaning only certain political positions and views are accepted. Therefore, how we are able to hear and engage with different positionings and perspectives is a core area of consideration for counselling psychologists given our diversity. How we as a profession and as individuals relate to such 'culture wars' issues is an area in which we may need to become bolder and clearer in the years to come. Research has shown us the way in which clients bring issues of electoral politics into the therapy room (Solomonov & Barber, 2018), and as counselling psychologists we need to be able to engage with this area of our work as sensitively and empathically as we do when clients tell us about their interpersonal difficulties at work. As discussed previously, a systems perspective is important to counselling psychology (see Chapter 4), and our social justice approach encourages us to consider the way in which our experience of the world is mediated by and located in various structures around us. In a world where talk of polarisation is increasing, alongside massive social and political instabilities globally, counselling psychologists must be bolder in their consideration of *how* precisely we engage with this part of our work. This will require reflection on our aims and agendas, along with sensitivity and compassion across differences.

Conclusion: deeds not words

As a profession, counselling psychology has made great strides over recent years in relation to social justice and anti-oppressive practices. However, given the histories of psychology and our complicity in various injustices, this progress was vitally needed and there was much to do. Therefore, this chapter has emphasised where we must become bolder and go beyond words, to act and to continue to address the much that is left to do. Anti-oppressive practice is not something which we can simply 'do' as a profession, and tick off our list. It is a process of becoming, of unlearning and relearning, of humility, of openness to our mistakes and our missteps, of disruption, of growth, and of action.

Reflexive questions

1 Cultural humility involves being fully open to the other, an awareness of our limitations, and a lifelong commitment to growth and
development. How do you feel when you think about being culturally humble? How easy or difficult might you find adopting this
attitude?
2 Imagine a situation in which you make an error in therapy in relation
to your clients' cultural identities (e.g. you offend them or hurt their
feelings), and there is a 'rupture' in the relationship. How would you
go about responding to this?

Critical thinking questions

1 In this chapter, we have considered three areas in which we think
counselling psychology can become bolder, in terms of anti-oppressive
practices. What other areas of anti-oppressive practice do you think the
field should develop?
2 When psychologists talk about working transculturally, some have
argued that as psychologists we need a wide-ranging knowledge and
understanding of cultures that are different from our own, so that
we always know about the different backgrounds and experiences
our clients come to us with. Do you agree? Why do you agree or
disagree?

Further reading and resources

• **The Black African and Asian Therapy Network** – https://www.
baatn.org.uk/
  This is an organisation which provides community for Counsellors
  and Psychotherapists of Black, African, Asian, and Caribbean Heritage in the UK, runs amazing events and conferences, and has many
  resources on its website which are exceptionally useful for all therapists
  and psychologists.
• **Psychologists for Social Change** – https://www.psychchange.
org/
  This is a network of applied psychologists and therapists, along with
  interested others, psychology graduates, and trainers who are interested in applying psychology to policy and political action. They have
  released policy briefings based on psychological research, run events
  and campaigns. They have various regional groups you can become
  involved in.
• **The Therapy and Social Change Network** – https://therapyand-
socialchange.net/

This provides a similar group to Psychologists for Social Change. They run regular events and meetings, and recordings of all their seminars are accessible via their website.

References

Alemohammad, S. (Mehdi). (2025). *It's time for psychologists to become activists*. BPS. https://www.bps.org.uk/psychologist/its-time-psychologists-become-activists

APA. (2021). *Apology to people of color for APA's role in promoting, perpetuating, and failing to challenge racism, racial discrimination, and human hierarchy in U.S.* https://www.apa.org. https://www.apa.org/about/policy/racism-apology

Auguste, E., Bowdring, M., Kasparek, S. W., McPhee, J., Tabachnick, A. R., Tung, I., & Galán, C. A. (2023). Psychology's contributions to anti-blackness in the United States within psychological research, criminal justice, and mental health. *Perspectives on Psychological Science, 18*(6), 1282–1305. https://doi.org/10.1177/17456916221141374

Beer, A. M., Spanierman, L. B., Greene, J. C., & Todd, N. R. (2012). Counseling psychology trainees' perceptions of training and commitments to social justice. *Journal of Counseling Psychology, 59*(1), 120–133. https://doi.org/10.1037/a0026325

Bemak, F., & Chung, R. C.-Y. (2008). New professional roles and advocacy strategies for school counselors: A multicultural/social justice perspective to move beyond the nice counselor syndrome. *Journal of Counseling & Development, 86*(3), 372–381. https://doi.org/10.1002/j.1556-6678.2008.tb00522.x

Brown, J. (2019). *Anti-oppressive counselling and psychotherapy*. Routledge.

Burman, E., Gowrisunkur, J., & Sangha, K. (1998). Conceptualizing cultural and gendered identities in psychological therapies. *European Journal of Psychotherapy & Counselling, 1*(2), 231–255. https://doi.org/10.1080/13642539808402311

Farrar, N., & Hanley, T. (2023). Where "culture wars" and therapy meet: Exploring the intersection between political issues and therapeutic practice. *Counselling and Psychotherapy Research, 23*(3), 593–597. https://doi.org/10.1002/capr.12623

Khalfan, A., Nilsson Lewis, A., Aguilar, C., Lawson, M., Jayoussi, S., Persson, J., Dabi, N., & Acharya, S. (2023). *Climate equality: A planet for the 99%*. Oxfam International. https://policy-practice.oxfam.org/resources/climate-equality-a-planet-for-the-99-621551/

Khan, M. (2023). *Working within diversity. A reflective guide to anti-oppressive practice in counselling and therapy*. Jessica Kingsley Publications.

Klein, N. (2014). *This changes everything: Capitalism vs. the climate*. Simon & Shuster.

Lago, C., & Smith, B. (Eds.). (2010). *Anti-discriminatory practice in counselling & psychotherapy*. Sage.

Milton, M. (2023). Therapy in the shadow of the climate and environmental crises. In L. A. Winter & D. Charura (Eds.), *The handbook of social justice in psychological therapies*. (pp. 163–175). Sage.

Mosher, D. K., Hook, J. N., Captari, L. E., Davis, D. E., DeBlaere, C., & Owen, J. (2017). Cultural humility: A therapeutic framework for engaging diverse clients. *Practice Innovations*, *2*(4), 221–233. https://doi.org/10.1037/pri0000055

Parker, I. (Ed.). (1999). *Deconstructing psychotherapy*. Sage.

Pilgrim, D. (1997). *Psychotherapy and society*. Sage.

Reeve, D. (2000). Oppression within the counselling room. *Disability & Society*, *15*(4), 669–682. https://doi.org/10.1080/09687590050058242

Saad, L. (2020). *Me and white supremacy: How to recognise your privilege, combat racism and change the world*. Quercus.

Solomonov, N., & Barber, J. P. (2018). Patients' perspectives on political self-disclosure, the therapeutic alliance, and the infiltration of politics into the therapy room in the Trump era. *Journal of Clinical Psychology*, *74*(5), 779–787. https://doi.org/10.1002/jclp.22609

Sue, D. W. (2001). Multidimensional facets of cultural competence. *The Counseling Psychologist*, *29*(6), 790–821. https://doi.org/10.1177/0011000001296002

Toporek, R., Gerstein, L., Fouad, N., Roysircar, G., & Israel, T. (Eds.). (2006). *Handbook for social justice in counseling psychology: Leadership, vision, and action*. Sage.

Tribe, R., & Bhugra, D. (Eds.). (2025). *Social justice, social discrimination, and mental health: Theory, practice, and professional issues*. Routledge. https://www.routledge.com/Social-Justice-Social-Discrimination-and-Mental-Health-Theory-Practice-and-Professional-Issues/Tribe-Bhugra/p/book/9781032395630

Turner, D. (2021). *Intersections of privilege and otherness in counselling and psychotherapy: Mockingbird*. Routledge.

Turner, D. (2023). *The psychology of supremacy: Imperium*. Routledge.

Turner, D. (2025). *Decolonising counselling and psychotherapy: Depoliticised pathways towards intersectional practice*. Routledge.

Winter, L. A., & Charura, D. (2023). An introduction to the handbook of social justice in psychological therapies. In L. A. Winter & D. Charura (Eds.), *The handbook of social justice in psychological therapies: Power, politics, change* (pp. 3–9). Sage.

Winter, L. A., & Hanley, T. (2015). "Unless everyone's covert guerilla-like social justice practitioners…": A preliminary study exploring social justice in UK counselling psychology. *Counselling Psychology Review*, *30*(2), 32–46.

Winter, L. A., Wood, M., & Shriberg, D. (2025). Practitioner psychologists as policy advocates, or policy as outside of our scope? Experiences and views of training in school and counseling psychology. *School Psychology International*, *46*(2), 153–171. https://doi.org/10.1177/01430343241305385

Index

Note: **Bold** page numbers refer to tables and *italic* page numbers refer to figures.

For Product Safety Concerns and Information please contact our EU
representative GPSR@taylorandfrancis.com
Taylor & Francis Verlag GmbH, Kaufingerstraße 24, 80331 München, Germany

www.ingramcontent.com/pod-product-compliance
Lightning Source LLC
Chambersburg PA
CBHW070421290526
45791CB00005B/1781